# HOME BREW

# HOME BREW

### Philip Ward

*Lyons & Burford, Publishers*

Library of Congress Cataloging-in-Publication Data

Ward, Philip, 1951-
    Home Brew / Philip Ward.
        p.    cm.
    Includes bibliographical references and index.
    ISBN 1-55821-315-5 (pbk.)
    1. Brewing – Amateur's manuals.    I. Title.
TP570.W27    1995
641.8.'73 – dc20                         95-19613
                                         CIP


Produced by AM Publishing Services
227 Park Avenue
Hoboken, NJ 07030
Illustrations: Patricia Shea
Design: Tony Meisel

Printed in the United States of America

10  9  8  7  6  5  4  3  2  1

# CONTENTS

*Once again, this book would not have been possible without Paula Marie.*
*You are an inspiration to me and to everyone you meet.*

# INTRODUCTION

*W*hat is it that has compelled so many diverse cultures to create so many different types and styles of a single, common beverage? Beer, like wine, has been with mankind for many centuries. A look at history explains how so many styles have evolved. Climatic conditions, environment, soil types, access to water and other factors have affected the types of beers that specific villages, regions and countries have created over the ages.

Like wine, seasonal weather changes have also played a large part in the creation of new beer styles. The brewer would plan his beverage processing well in advance so that the proper beer would be ready for the weather. As temperatures became colder, a brewer would make richer and more full-bodied beers – stouts, ales and the like. Conversely, a light, refreshing Pilsener or wheat beer would be just right for the heat of summer.

Many people became home brewers out of necessity because potable water was scarce – the brewing process results in a mostly homogenized beverage. Besides being an alternative source of liquid to the tainted city waters of the ancients, beer has a low alcohol content making it an ideal drinking water substitute.

Brewing beer at home has become a huge business in contemporary America with home brew shops sprouting up in almost every city. Most of these shops will also sell the ingredients necessary to get started by mail order. Unlike wine, which can take months or years to fully process, homemade beer can be ready to drink in less than a month from start-up. With modern technology, your first batch (properly brewed, of course) will probably be as good as most commercially available beers and you have the satisfaction of knowing that you crafted it yourself.

Along with the rising popularity of home brewing in America has come the rise of the micro-brewery and the brew pub. Without question, these institutions are here to stay and are veritable meccas for the beer enthusiast. However, they're also less than great bargains, with $3.50 the typical price for a brew pub pint and micro six-packs retailing for $5 *at the very least*. So along with having a whole lot of fun when simulating your favorite brews at home, you also reduce the cost of your beer adventures in the process.

# 1
# BEERS OF
# THE WORLD

Most experts believe that beer making began when once-nomadic peoples settled down and began to grow crops. Barley is the first recorded grain used to brew a beverage with an alcoholic kick. The Egyptians, Mesopotamians and Sumerians are all pictured working with barley to produce beer. In its first form it was certainly a rough-and-tumble version of what we know as beer, but it is the basis for what home brewers are still striving for – an easily prepared, good tasting brew.

Like grapes – the basis for wine – barley, wheat and other grains were simple to cultivate and had multiple uses. They could be used to feed a farmer's animals and his family and to create spirited beverages. The once-nomadic farmer could convert these agricultural products quite easily and the end results could be lucrative and sustaining. Through experimentation, the farmer could enhance the quality of his crops to create a higher-priced product or to produce better quality animals. Such adjustments could also result in a better brew.

It is thought that the first brews were probably produced from breads mixed with other flavorings. In fact, the Anchor

Brewing Company of San Francisco set out to recreate one of the ancient recipes a few years ago using bread combined with fruits and honey and a cultivated yeast instead of what surely would have been a wild yeast in the old times. The result was palatable and had interesting flavor according to the accounts of this experiment into brewing's history.

Brewing spread rapidly throughout Europe. The center of brewing then, as today, was the northern part of the continent. In southern Europe, it was possible to cultivate the grains necessary for brewing, but it was also easy to grow the favored crop, grapes. The church needed wine for its religious ceremonies, permitted the flock to consume it at leisure and also dominated the production and ownership of many vineyards.

The north, however, lacked the fruit necessary to make wine of any quality. Folks there still needed to relax from time to time and they found that the grains necessary for beer making could be grown in their northerly clime. The one exception was Germany which is fortunate enough to have micro-climates resulting in world-class wines and wonderful beer.

Brewing styles evolved and specific types of beer – ales, lagers, pilseners, stouts, etc. – were created for different times of the year and for varying styles of foods. Production also began to change with technological advances and the rising popularity of beer. Commercial breweries thus began to spring up in cities of all sizes. There were still the farmers making beer for themselves and their extended families, but more and more people began to rely on the brewer-tradesman's product. Standardization of styles steadily developed and home brewing for city dwellers became an anomaly.

In America, there was extensive commercial production of beer of all styles before Prohibition. Thousands of family-owned breweries thrived with douncesens in every city and region of the United States. When Prohibition arrived, most of the smaller breweries quickly failed during the period from 1920 to 1933. Only the strongest and most innovative breweries survived by directing their production towards other industries. When Prohibition was revoked, there was still much trepidation within the beer and wine industries and they needed a way to appeal to a larger market. Slowly but surely, they realized they must make beers that were less strong and lighter in color and flavor, to broaden their appeal with the American public.

When World War II arrived and most of the male citizenry went off to war, women became the primary market for the large breweries. They felt it essential to produce beers that would be appreciated by the "gentler" sex and the American pilsener style of beer became the industry norm. To this day, this light style of beer is still America's favorite – witness the popularity of Budweiser, Coors, Miller, Rolling Rock and hundreds more. It is certainly understandable that this style would prevail given our warmer temperatures for almost six months of the year. What has astonished many observers is that when the weather gets cooler, Americans traditionally do not switch to heavier styles of beer, as they do in other countries.

In the past fifteen to twenty years, there has been a quiet revolution taking hold of the commercial beer industry – the development of micro-breweries and brew pubs. This movement was spurred on by the baby boomers and their boredom with the lighter beers of the previous generation. They were searching for careers in alternative industries, knew they enjoyed a good beer when they tasted it and began to research why and how these beers were more interesting to consume.

One of these pioneers was Jack MacAuliffe who fell in love with quality brews in Britain and returned home to Sonoma, California, to create the first micro-brewery, New Albion, in the mid 1970s. His revolution against the large brewers was quickly followed by others of like mind and micro-breweries can now be found throughout the United States. As this change began to take hold of the beer industry, the consuming public began to realize that making quality beer at home was also very easy and a lot cheaper than paying premium prices for micro-brews. With modern technology, it is as easy as reading directions, opening a can, adding water and having patience to create beers of the quality and flavor of some of the best commercial brews.

## TYPES AND STYLES OF BEERS

This portion will identify and describe the varieties and types of beer available throughout the world. Within each type, class or family of beer there can be many different off-shoots and variations – more than we can do justice to in one book.

Most beer consumed worldwide is probably of the lighter ale or Pilsener-style lager because of the delicate aromas and flavors and the relatively low alcohol content (under 5 percent). These brews are perfect for consumption in the warm months and with the lighter food associated with this time of year. We begin this chapter with the lighter lagers and will move up the scale to the richer styles.

Most of the beers in this section are suited for home brewing. It may take some practice to create the type you desire and also some research to locate the necessary grains, hops, malt, etc. Right now, we will not get into the specifics of the brewing process – terms of measuring alcohol, depth of color and other more pertinent terminology that is essential to learn. All of this will be found in upcoming chapters. The following information will help spark ideas and help you better appreciate the many types of beer that have been created throughout the history of brewing. Once you have an understanding and, hopefully, a taste of some of these beers, you will develop your own preferences and before long wish to create your own home brews.

*LAGERS*: Lager (German for *storeroom*) is always aged for a period of time before being sold or consumed. The amount of time the beer is aged depends on the ingredients and the final taste desired. Once a cool fermentation is finished, the beer is allowed to rest in its fermentation container at low temperatures (around 32° F) for up to three months or as little as two weeks. Lagers, because of their cool fermentation, typically have special yeasts fermenting at the bottom of the fermentation vessel.

The concept of aging the beer was conceived because brewers of yore found that, when stored at low temperatures, beer would not spoil even in the heat of summer. They also found that the beer became stabilized, like wine does, at these low temperatures. Once bottled, the beer tasted clean and refreshing and would not improve with any bottle aging. In fact, its quality often began to deteriorate.

When lagers were first produced, all were of the dark variety. Then a brewer in the town of Pilsen in Bohemia (now part of the Czech Republic) brewed a golden lager that caught the attention of the drinking public. It became, over the years, the standard model for America's brewing giants. One of the neighboring villages was called Budweis, and the town had long produced a pilsener-style lager called Budweiser. The Anheuser-Busch Brewery in St. Louis later created a beer in this style and named it Budweiser. It is, to this day, the American version of what was (and still is) a wonderful European lager, Pilsener Urquell.

Golden lagers of this style have a lovely, light-golden color, good malt characteristics, a light hoppiness and sometimes even a citrus, apple-scented aroma. What made the difference between the original pilsener and other lagers of the time was the use of the soft local water, specific hops still grown in the area and specific yeast strains. Even today, many breweries, wishing to emulate the style of the original, purchase their hops from the Czech Republic.

Dortmünder-style lagers are quite similar to a pilsener with the same dryness and light-golden color though perhaps less aromatic. The style has become difficult to find but there are a few micro-breweries making Dortmünder.

The Bavaria region is generally regarded as the home of the dark lager style that preceded the pilsener style. Documented production of this type dates as far back as 500 B.C. Production of these dark lagers was centered in the town of Kulmbach and to this day most people in the industry call such lagers "Bavarian." Many commercial brewers make a dark lager—even Anheuser-Busch with its Michelob Classic Dark. The classic attributes of dark lagers are beautiful, dark amber to brown color, aromas of coffee and notes of hoppiness and yeast. The flavors will be quite rich with follow-through from the aromatics.

Dark lagers are a good bet for home brewers beacuse all of the necessary ingredients are readily available at supply stores.

Vienna, Marzen and Oktoberfest styles of lager are all very similar. It is generally agreed that the Vienna style was developed first and then brewers began to change the style to meet the demands of the March and October festivals. This also allowed the brewers to "lager" the beers for a period of time to develop the nuances that the consuming public was looking for in this style of beer.

Today the styles are still varied depending on the brewer, but generally they share a lovely, amber-red color with a sweetish malt flavor even leaning toward a toffee/caramel note. Many American micro-breweries are producing beers in this style and three of them are well distributed on the East Coast: New Amsterdam and Albany Amber of New York and Portland Lager from Maine. These three beers are slightly different but have that hint of palate sweetness and attractive amber color in common.

Bock beers are lagers that are fermented cool, aged and usually consumed during the cooler months of the year. They have a dark amber color, lovely rich taste with a sweet maltiness. Because they traditionally ferment longer, their alcohol content is around 6 percent by volume and some double bocks can approach 7 percent by volume. These rich lagers are perfect for the richer foods of the winter months and some of the more full-bodied bocks can even be paired with desserts.

For the home brewer, lagering may be difficult because it requires storing the finished beer at 32°F (or as close to this as possible) for a minimum of three weeks and for as long as two to three months. Most people don't have the refrigeration to accommodate a container or the patience, but if you are inclined to try, you won't be disappointed with the resulting brew.

*ALES*: Fortunately, the term ale has been rejoined to its true meaning in America due to the quality of ales being produced here as well as accessibility of high-quality, imported brews. One of the great misnomers prevailing in a few of the states to this day is the designation of any beer over 4 percent alcohol as an ale. Prior to the rebirth of quality ale, many beers were labeled ales, but in fact bore no resemblance to a true European-style ale.

Within the ale category there are many different styles; hang in there as we touch on the most popular of the many.

As a group, ales are typically fermented at quite warm temperatures (56°F to 76°F) as compared to the cool fermentation of lagers. This warmer fermentation keeps the yeasts at the top of the fermenter, hence most ales are known as "top-fermented" beers. Ales are aged after completion of fermentation, and the aging process will vary with the style of ale that is brewed.

Mild, bitters (also known as session ales) and pale ales are all quite similar and most discussions try to define how each of these differ, if at all. Many British commercial brewers produce a mild *and* a bitter *and* a pale.

The general impression of milds is that they are an easy drink for the (often working class) pub-goer. Mild ales have a tendency toward lower alcohol content, softer flavors and run the gamut from pale to dark in color. Bitters are what one will find poured from the draft tap in most pubs and is the everyday drink of the typical consumer of ales in the British Islands. The flavors lean toward a stronger hop characteristic and a touch more bitterness than a mild. Like many beer-related issues, most would agree that the difference between mild and bitter ale is subtle and depends on one's personal taste. And every brewer has feelings about what the qualitative differences are and will interpret them in his or her own fashion.

Then there are the pale ales. Most are certainly not pale in color and usually have an amber-red hue (though they are certainly lighter in color than stouts or porters). Most producers feel that the ale should have just a "blush" of color (not to be confused with the pink hue of blush wine) – a light-bronze or golden hue. Some believe that pales have a nuttier quality whereas bitters will be a little drier in the finish due to the particular hops utilized. But, after all is said, there is no real definition of pale ales because every brewer has his own interpretation.

India pale ale (I.P.A.) is a subcategory of pales developed in England during colonial days. Its name was derived from the style of ales that ended their journeys being consumed in India by English emigrants. The ales were produced in England, shipped by boat in wooden casks and subjected to major temperature changes and the rolling action of the sea. Those who consumed the ales in India felt that the quality of the ales had been much improved by their arduous journeys. Today there are very few India Pale Ales produced commercially in England and most of the American versions are made by micro-breweries. Of the commercial I.P.A.s, Ballantine (now brewed by Pabst) is the most widely available. As with most styles of beer and ale, the final result will be up to the brewer's interpretation. India Pales have a hoppy characteristic, light body and a color of light to golden amber with a refreshing palate feel.

Scottish ales are usually richer in color and flavor than their counterparts in England. This style developed from the type of malts used to produce them. They are darker in color, leaning toward a light mahogany. The bouquet and flavor of Scottish ale includes notes of malt, sometimes a roasted barley/nut/peat edge, a distinct hoppiness and traditionally a smoky character.

Irish ales have been overlooked by most people due to the popularity of the other famous Irish brews, porter and stout. Irish ales have a distinct reddish hue and malty flavor with a touch of sweetness that is quite appealing. Most of the breweries in Ireland that produce these ales are owned by the Guinness Company and are rarely exported. If you are looking for an American version to taste, the Coors Brewery has been licensed to use the name of George Killian.

Brown ales constitute another very popular style. These ales were developed in the Newcastle area of England and had a lighter brown-amber color to differentiate them from the darker beers and lighter ales of the times. Being true ales they are top fermented and typically have a richer, sweeter taste and texture. The color is quite pleasant and inviting in the glass. For home brewers who have never experienced a brown, there are two very good commercial examples widely available in the United States: Pete's Wicked Ale (U.S.A.) and Newcastle Nut Brown Ale (England). Recognized as a leader in the revolution in American brewing, Pete's is considered a decidedly Americanized version of brown ale. Many find brown ale quite easy to recreate in the home brewery and the resulting ales can be very rewarding.

Wheat beers are classically made with the same type of yeasts as other ales—they ferment at the top of the vessel. What differentiates wheat beer from its peers in the beer family is, naturally enough, the high proportion of wheat in the mash. There are also special yeasts for wheat beer and yeastiness is among the flavors traditionally associated with this singular group.

There are many different styles of wheat beers; the best originated and are still produced, in Germany, both in the south and the north. Wheat beers are known as weissbier or weizenbier depending on the recipe, where it is made and to whom you are talking. Weisse means white and describes the color of the foaming action that is visible during wheat beer's fermentation (versus the darker foam of a barley-based beer's fermentation). Weizenbier means wheat beer and describes the wheat that is used as the base for the beer. Look also for the word *hefe* (yeast) on the label – a hefeweiss or a weissbier *mit hefe* (with yeast) will have decidedly strong notes of yeast. Many wheat beer drinkers are yeast-lovers, even rolling their bottles gently across a table to stir up the yeast sediment before opening them.

Wheat beers will have a clovelike character along with the distinctive yeasty aroma and flavor profile. They are ideal in the warm summer months, and they are known for their crisp and refreshing acidity as well.

Belgian ales cover the gamut of styles. If you have the luck or wherewithal to travel to this lovely country, you're in for some wonderful beer and ale drinking. Ale is brewed in all of the nine provinces of Belgium, the styles varying with the region of production. Because of its northerly location, it was difficult for Belgians to produce wine grapes of any quality, so the residents have put all of their effort into producing some of the world's best brews. Belgian beers are often not listed as ales but they are definitely made in an ale style—most of them are top fermenting. There are at least five distinct styles of Belgian ales and we will do our best to give you some qualitative impressions about them.

The classic Belgian ale has a wonderful golden-brown color, a malty flavor balanced by delicate hoppy characteristics and is a very refreshing beverage on a warm day. The main flavor and aromatic profile of these ales comes from unique yeast strains plus the addition of small amounts of hops. Belgian browns are produced from barley and have a distinct, hoppy, light character. The color is on the dark side and the beauty of these brews is that the best of them will age well like fine wine. Producers may allow their browns to age for up to six months in the bottle before releasing them for sale. They are typically sold in sparkling wine-type bottles.

Saison-style ales were and still are produced by small artisanal producers. They were thought in years past to be rustic in style, but the quality is now remarkably good. Among the most widely available is Saison Dupont which has a lovely, golden-brown color, appealing aromas of barley and fruit and slight herbaceousness. The taste is quite full and marries well with foods. These brews, due to their artisanal crafting, do throw some sediment from the remaining yeast cells and if you want an interesting flavor addition be sure to finish every drop.

Red ales have a dark amber, almost red wine color and are considered the most thirst quenching of all Belgian ales. The color might make you anticipate a heavy beer, but

Belgian reds are actually light in body with well-balanced flavor.

Trappist ales are made exclusively at six monasteries in Belgium and the Netherlands. The style has developed over the centuries and the main characteristic they all share is top fermentation and bottle conditioning. In taste and color there are definite differences, but they share a golden to dark amber color, and full, rich flavors that are even sweet at times. Ample in alcohol and body, all leave a yeast sediment from the old world brewing techniques. These wonderful beers can be consumed with a broad spectrum of foods.

Bière de Garde ales were created in the north of France in the region that borders Belgium and are still made by small producers in both countries. These beers were created by artisanal farmer/brewers to age in wood casks for consumption in the summer months. Today, the tradition continues and the ales are sold in Champagne bottles with wire hoods. They will improve with some bottle conditioning and they all have some sediment from the yeast cells that remain after the fermentation. The beers were typically top fermented (now many are bottom fermented) with light and dark malts. Color ranges from a full golden to a darkish red amber. They have wonderful flavors replete with malt and spiciness.

Barley wine is, of course, not a wine at all but a type of ale that typically is quite high in alcohol content (6 percent to 13 percent) and usually served at the end of a meal. The color of the brew can range from amber to a lovely mahogany. The aromatics are somewhat winey, with undertones of ripe fruits (cherries, apples), malt and hops. Impressions on the palate include a full and round flavor – a sweet quality with cream and citrus notes balanced by good acidity and strength from the high alcohol content. Barley wines are sometimes aged in oak casks for a slow maturation and to add complexity to their already heady style. Some brewers will even stir the yeasts that precipitate to the bottom of the barrel back into the brew. Most barley winemakers use an ale yeast for their fermentations but some may use a wine yeast in combination with the ale yeast to add yet another component to the resulting brew. It was once believed that ale yeasts would not be able to complete the alcoholic fermentations necessary to reach a barley wine level. There are, however, specific ale yeast strains that will complete a fermentation up to 14 percent alcohol.

For the home brewer wishing to produce barley wine, the main problem is cost – ingredients for an extract-based, good-quality barley wine will cost about $60 for a 5-gallon batch. And of course, patience must be a virtue, as it will take a minimum of one year for the brew to be properly bottle conditioned. Some recent tasting notes in a trade publication were astounding. The first "vintage" of Eldridge and Pope's "Thomas Hardy" barley wine dated 1969 (!) was sampled at a luncheon in Pennsylvania. Interestingly, it was considered, by many, to be better than four or five other vintages tasted the same day. So, you see, it does take a long time for this brew to mature and develop!

There are many other styles of ales produced throughout the world, but they are generally thought to be less prominent. For example, there is a new American style of ale. It is usually quite floral due to the use of hops that have been grown in Washington and Oregon states. This style is still in development and evolving slowly, but it is distinctly American. Be sure to discuss this with your local brew pub or home brew supply shop.

*PORTERS AND STOUTS*: These two very heavy, dark breeds get their color and richness from malts and barleys that are roasted almost like espresso or French roast coffee beans. They are usually made in the top fermenting style as an ale would be and this may add some lightness. We will address porters first, but then again differentiation between styles is sometimes difficult. Indeed, it was extra-strong, *stout* porter that was later shortened to become just "stout."

Porters were first developed outside London in the 1730s as a beer to be consumed by porters (hence the name) and laborers. It was felt the brew would give them sustenance to finish their day's labor. The recipe was once based on darkly roasted, unmalted barley with a small amount of licorice added. In current recipes the licorice has been deleted but the barley and (now) malts are still roasted quite dark. Porter was eventually taken over in popularity by stout and at one point there were no porters brewed at all in the British Isles.

The brew revolution in the America and Britain has brought about a renewed interest in porters and there are now several brands available. Porter is quite dark with toffee and coffee notes in the color as well as in the aroma. The flavor leans toward a bitter taste, but is balanced by the rich flavors of the dark roasting.

Stouts, on the other hand, have never fallen out of favor and are considered by many to have a beneficial quality to the human body. Stout's most famous producer is of course the Guinness Brewery of Dublin, Ireland. Stout and porter were both produced by Guinness and their porter once even surpassed stout as their most popular brew. But now it is stout that has made this company so successful and respected within the beverage industry. As with porter, the best stouts are top fermented, made from roasted barleys and have a roasted chocolatelike aroma and flavor.

Stout's hoppiness may have originated from necessity. Larger quantities of hops would allow the brews to stabilize and maintain the secondary fermentation over the winter and spring months. When there was no refrigeration, brewers kept their wares in cellars, but at times it still was not cold enough to keep out certain bacteria. The yeast strain *Brettanomyces* developed from the addition of the hops and the long secondary fermentation and acted as a protectant. It also added that attractive bitter and acidic quality that we have come to expect and enjoy from a well-made stout. Also, Guinness allows a certain percentage of their stout to actually sour and then blends this portion back into the master blend.

Sweet ("milk" and "cream" versions) and imperial stouts are variations on the theme. Sweet stouts were developed to capitalize on the popularity of stouts and to make up for a lack of calories and carbohydrates in nineteenth-century England. The stouts had the addition of milk lactose and they did seem to have a creaminess. There are a few commercial brews of this style available today and most still add a small amount of lactose (milk sugar) at the end of the process for the sweet edge. The dark color and light toffee-colored head come from the malts used.

Another type of sweet stout that has been reborn is based on the addition of oats to the brewing process. Among the most widely available is Samuel Smith's of England. Most oatmeal stouts have less than 10 percent oat product in them. Look to them for a creamy feel with hints of roasted coffee and toffee aromas. They are wonderful with desserts containing cream, coffee or nuts. The drawback with oats for the home brewer is that they are very difficult to work with.

Imperial stouts were originally developed to be shipped to the Baltics and Russia where they were much appreciated because of the cold winters and the brews' ability to warm the body. In some people's minds, imperial stouts and barley wines are considered interchangeable. But a taste test will reveal definite differences between these two ales. The characteristics of the full-bodied imperial include roasted nuts and coffee, maybe even hot cocoa, and a fruit quality that seems to resemble a blackberry tart fresh from the oven. It will also have the sweetness of a rich sherry or a Madeira made from the Bual grape. As you can see from the description, this is not a beverage to be taken lightly. It is perfect for a cold winter night, a fireplace, wonderful companionship and a lovely dessert.

There are many more beers, ales, lagers, pilseners and variations and combinations thereof – all of which could be discussed at great length. Armed with this basic know-how, you can now explore on your own – talk up beer styles and recipes at your home brew supply store. Take home an assortment of "singles" from your beer retailer for tasting, and read everything you can get your hands on about the world's harvest of beer.

# 2
# *THE HOME BREWERY*

*A*s a home winemaker would, so should the home brewer: find a place to brew and a place for storage and go to it. That may be a bit of a simplification, but for starters you do need a work area (kitchen) and a quiet spot for the beer to sit and work its magic.

You should read all of this chapter (and all of this book) before you run out and spend any of your hard-earned money on equipment. And start simply, with a basic brew, before moving to more complex recipes and styles. Anyone reasonably able to follow instructions can accomplish a good-tasting and inexpensive brew on the first attempt.

When you go to make that first brew supply purchase, talk to the storekeeper about your wishes and listen to his advice. Most of the men and women in the home brewing business have a keen (even devotional) interest in brewing and are always willing to make recommendations. Besides spreading their "faith," your beer making success will create a repeat customer for them.

Your kitchen or other area that has a stove, sink, tabletop

and work space will be your main area of operation for the brewing process. If you have the inclination and the good fortune of available space, do set up a specific area for beer making because the process can be rather messy.

It will take about an hour from the boiling of the wort (i.e., the mixture of ingredients that eventually becomes beer, pronounced *wert*) to the beginning of fermentation. Make certain that all equipment is clean and sanitized and in good working order. The cleanliness is mandatory to keep any unwanted bacterial infections or wild yeasts out of your brew. Bacterial problems can spoil a perfectly good batch of beer in no time at all.

Once the brew has been completed, it will be necessary to find a good location for bottling. This area should be well lighted, clean and offer room to set up your miniature bottling plant. Again, if you have an area that was specifically designed as your home brewery, then you are all set. Otherwise, use the basement floor, garage or an outside shed. The bottling process can get messy, too.

Following is a list of equipment that that you'll need to create your beer. Some of this equipment will not be used with a basic brew, but it is good to know what you may need down the road when you broaden your scope of expertise in the world of home brewing. Most home brew supply shops and kitchen equipment stores will have the ingredients you need to complete this shopping list. Special order or shop by catalogue for anything you cannot find from a local retailer. The list will allow you to make about 5 gallons of beer at one time. You can buy larger quantities or more equipment as you need it.

*enamel stock pot with lid*

*Basics*

- 4-, 5- or 6-gallon stainless steel or enamel *stock pot with a lid*. From kitchen/restaurant supply shops or check your existing pot supply (lobster pots are perfect).

- 5- or 6-gallon glass *carboy*. Find these at your beer/wine making supply shop.

    *or*

- 5- or 6-gallon *food grade* (and marked as such) *plastic fermenting container* that can accept an airlock and also has a lid that is tight fitting. Buy from your home brew shop or recycle one from a restaurant or cafeteria – but wash it spotlessly clean and *avoid* buckets scratched on the insides which are *unsanitary*.

- 5- or 10-gallon *plastic bucket/trash container*. Same criteria as above.

- 5, 6 or 7 feet of *clear plastic tubing*, ideally ³⁄₈-inch outside diameter. This will be used for transferring your beer from one vessel to another. The brew supply shop will have lots of this.

- *Air/fermentation lock* and the proper rubber stopper

carboy with air/fermentation lock

fermentation bucket with lid and airlock

(carboy users only) to accommodate the air lock. This will be used during the fermentation process to allow carbon dioxide to escape and to keep harmful air out. From your home brew shop.

- An assortment of bottle and carboy *brushes* to enable you to clean your containers. Grocery stores and home brew shops have these.

- A *bottle capper* and lots of *caps*. Caps must be new and unused "blanks" (they're flat). From your home brew shop.

- About forty-eight *refillable* 12-ounce beer *bottles*, long-necks, *nonscrew top only*, or twenty-four 22-ounce bottles. Do not

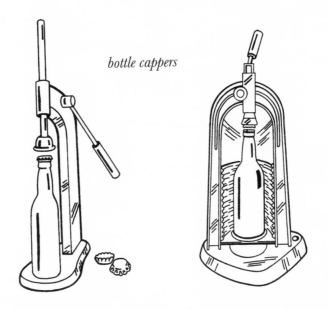

*bottle cappers*

use basic, screw-top nonrefillable bottles which are made of thinner glass and are liable to explode when filled with home brew. Good bottles can be found at the local brew supply or recycling/redemption center. With the latter approach especially, make sure the bottles are *very* clean and sanitized before putting your home brew into them.

- For recycling, nothing beats the coveted flip-cap bottles used by Grolsch, Fischer and a few other European makers. Not only are they made of good, thick glass and large enough to hold lots of beer, they also eliminate the capping process. Home brew suppliers even sell replacement rubber gaskets for these bottles. So stock up on these excellent brands for your own consumption or befriend the owner of the redemption center.

*beer bottles*

Alternately:

- Twenty-five sparkling wine/Champagne bottles that are able to accept bottlecaps. Most of them will, but check first. European wine bottles usually will not work with our bottlecaps – stick with American or Canadian-made bottles. Check beer or winemaking suppliers or recycle from home, friends or restaurants. Again, make sure they are squeaky clean before using them. Serving your home brew from this type of bottle adds a note of festivity to your table, plus it means fewer bottles to cap.

- A *hydrometer* from the home brew supply store. An essential piece of equipment, the hydrometer is used to measure the amount of sugar in the unfermented wort and to monitor the progress of the fermenting brew. (Fermentation is the conversion of sugar to alcohol – it will be explained in the next chapter.) Read the hydrometer's directions carefully and review its use with your home brew retailer. A small tube or jar – usually sold with a hydrometer – is used to extract a small amount of wort and hold it for testing.

Besides measuring specific gravity, hydrometers also read degrees of Balling/Plato and potential alcohol level. Balling/

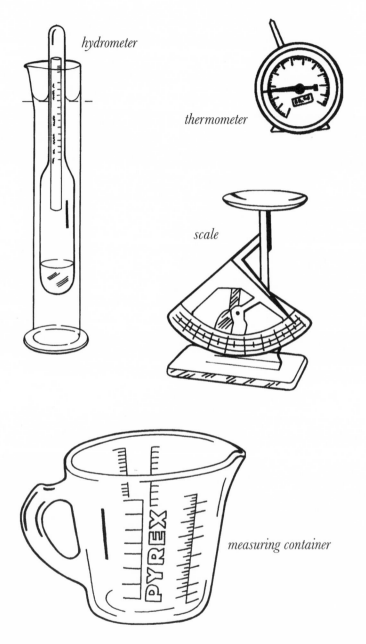

*hydrometer*

*thermometer*

*scale*

*measuring container*

Plato is used by intermediate brewers and is derived from the specific gravity. Potential alcohol level is also a useful measurement for the home brewer. When you take the initial reading from your wort prior to the addition of the yeast, make sure to record it in your journal (see page 34). Then take the final reading after fermentation is finished, just prior to bottling. Subtract the lower number (the last reading) from the higher number (the first reading) and you will be able to determine the approximate alcohol level of your home brew. Now you will be able to answer the inevitable question posed by friends sampling your home brew: "How much alcohol is in it?"

- *Thermometer* with a range of 32° to 212°F or O° to 100°C. Look for a thermometer that is of the dial type with degrees marked off in 1-degree increments. Check the home brew supply shop or hardware store.

- A *scale* able to accommodate up to 16 ounces. These are becoming less necessary as many brew supply stores now weigh ingredients for their customers.

- A Pyrex/glass *measuring container* that will allow for measurements of up to 1 quart of liquid.

- A large stainless steel *spoon* or any spoon that you can sterilize. This will be used to stir up the wort. Many brew supply shops recommend plastic, food grade, paddle-style stirrers

*stainless steel spoon*

that are easily sterilized. A wooden spoon won't do.

- Chlorine *bleach or sanitizing products* formulated to be environmentally safe. The best known is B-Brite™. This will ensure that all of your equipment will be clean. (Grocery store/brew supply shop.)
- If possible, a *refrigerator* that you can use for water, beer and brewing supplies; of a size that will accommodate the fermenting brew.
- A *notebook* or *journal* that you will use to record recipes and all of the specifics of your brewing process. It is essential to keep accurate records to make a consistently great brew.

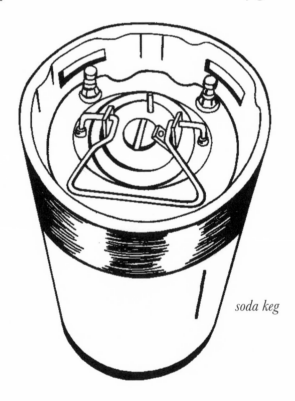

*soda keg*

*For Advanced Brewing*

- Mesh *straining bags* from the home brew supply shop. Used for specialty brews that call for malt grains. Like a teabag, it allows you to steep the grains without having to strain the liquid.
- *Quarter keg or a used soda dispensing container (soda keg).* This equipment is a bit more expensive, but it's nice to have only one vessel to sanitize instead of forty-eight bottles. These are also very simple to clean and to use for dispensing your brew. Kegs and dispensers are especially great if you are having a party for people who appreciate a good brew.
- A *mash tun* – used by the all-grain brewer to mash grains to create the wort.
- *Wort chiller* to aid in the speedy chilling of the wort. These are commercially available and also the ingenious brewer can fashion his own from heater hosing and copper tubing.
- A *lauter tun* is mandatory for the all-grain brewer. Again, they are commercially available, but the handy brewer can fashion one using a little ingenuity and some common sense.
- A *filter system* to be used to rid your brew of bacteria and yeast sediment, and reduce the potential for "chill haze" (more later). With costs declining, these filtration systems are becoming more popular for the advanced brewery. Replacement filters are a bit expensive – beware.
- A *water filtration system* – if you live in an area that has water that has been heavily treated.
- A *brew belt* is a fine tool for those wanting to monitor the temperature during the fermentation process. These are plastic-coated belts that encircle the fermenting vessel and plug into a normal wall socket. They are preset at about 72°F to 75°F and are great for cool-weather brewing.

There are other pieces of equipment that you will need to craft different styles and types of beers, but this list will help you on your way nicely.

Most brew supply shops have made it very simple to get started. They offer basic brew kits that include all the necessary equipment to begin the adventure of creating the great beers of the world. One such kit might include a fermentation bucket and lid, an air/fermentation lock, siphon hoses, a hydrometer, a capper, bottle brush, sanitizing equipment, bottling bucket and a bottling filler tip, bottlecaps and a thermometer. The only thing you need is to decide what style of beer you wish to create. This type of starter kit is ideal for the beginner and usually costs under $75.

A kit reduces the cost of having to buy all of the equipment separately and will allow you to begin brewing at a dramatically reduced cost. Once you have this basic equipment you can make wonderful beer for years to come. The initial cost can certainly be amortized over many home brews.

Whenever you are setting out to brew, make certain that you have everything you need, that all of your equipment is in working order, that all of your containers are clean and that you have all the ingredients called for on hand.

# 3
# *BASIC HOME BREWING*

*B*rewing is based on the science of fermentation – changing sugar into alcohol. The way we accomplish this is by adding little yeast cells that like to eat sugar and lovingly convert it into alcohol. Unfortunately, the yeast cells die after they have performed their wonderful task and then must be removed from the fermenting vessel. That's a pretty simple explanation of a quite complicated process, but essentially that is what happens with beer as well as wine. With wine we are converting the sugars in grapes into an alcoholic beverage; with beer we are changing the sugars in malted barley ("malt") into the beverage.

Most beginning home brewers will start with a kit that includes the ingredients needed to make a batch of beer. The brewer need only add water and the yeast and malt extract as directed. Note how simple it has become to create a great brew! Modern technology and mankind's thirst for a good home brew has made this once difficult process so easy. Many ways exist to enhance your brew with the addition of special malts, hops and grains; this chapter will give you the basics.

Almost all home brew supply shops have made the brewing process quite simple by making available fail-safe recipes and ingredient packages. A fine example would be a "best bitter" recipe package that would include crystal malt, dry malt, malt extract, Fuggles and Goldings hops, ale yeast, priming sugar and cheese cloth (or a mesh bag). Talk about simple, good and cheap! Such a package retails for around $25 and makes 5 gallons of ale. That comes to 50 cents for a 12-ounce bottle of your *own* brew. You have both the pleasure of knowing you are saving many dollars and the sublime pleasure of creating your own beer.

## THE BASIC BREWING PROCESS

By using a prehopped malt extract package you can make a fine beer your first time out of the gate. It is the simplest way and you will only need to follow some basic instructions. The process is as follows and will be explained in more detail shortly.

First, to make the malt extract less viscous, place it in a warm water bath for about 15 minutes. Then follow the directions on the label concerning the length of time recommended for the prehopped malt extract. *Exception*: some books and home brew kits suggest adding corn sugar to the wort in lieu of a malt "kicker" (extra malt to boost fermentation) but all brewers and brew shops in the know warn against it – they will demand that you use malt extract.

Secondly, put the remaining clean cold water (that you were unable to fit into your pot) into your sanitized, rinsed fermenter, then add the wort (malt extract and water mixture) to the fermenter. Take a reading with your hydrometer.

When the temperature of the liquid mixture has reached

about 78°F, you may add your yeast and attach the fermentation lock.

A few days later, confirm that primary fermentation has been completed using your hydrometer.

Finally, rack your beer, prime your beer, bottle it, cap it, condition it and of course drink your first home brew.

Congratulations on a new achievement and the beginning of a newfound talent!

Now it really *can* be that simple and that is why so many people have made the move to brewing.

Now we'll begin looking in greater detail at all of the steps above. Read – and reread until you understand – this whole chapter before attempting your first home brew.

The prehopped malt extract that you will use has been formulated to make brewing quite easy. We will discuss malting in an upcoming portion of the book but suffice it to say that it's an elaborate process that requires the proper work environment to make great malt. There are many different types and styles of malt extract brew kits available from around the world. They offer the home brewer the opportunity to make brews from England, Australia, Ireland, Scotland, Germany and the United States. Virtually any beer you can imagine – from American "light" to Belgian *peche* (peach) to Imperial stout can be found in kit form.

By the way, brew shops often recommend not using the yeast which is included in the malt kit. They suggest using good, fresh yeast (which they'll sell you, of course) for a better brew.

Malts are made from specific grains, mostly barley, that give definite flavor and aromatic components to the finished product. The selected barley is then allowed to germinate and

*bottle and carboy brushes
are necessary to ensure clean receptacles*

*rinsing out the carboy*

then is dried. The barley germination and drying process develops soluble starch, sugar and enzymes which convert starch to sugar. The variety of barley used, the germination period, kilning (drying) time and the kiln temperature will affect the quality of the malt extract. This in turn will affect the aroma, flavor, body, and head retention of the resultant beer, as well as the fermenting ability of the water and malt mixture (wort).

Every producer of these malt extracts has an interpretation of what a pale, pilsener, bitter or stout should taste like. Experiment and find one that suits your palate.

Once you have dissolved the malt extract in the water, you have made a basic wort. (The wort is your beginning and it may be adjusted by adding other grains or adjuncts to change the flavors. But for now let's just stick with the basics.) After it has come to boil, let it boil, vigorously, for 15 minutes or more (check the label or recipe) to allow for a full blending and slight reduction of the volume of the liquid.

Before beginning, you should have cleaned and sanitized all of the equipment that will come into contact with the wort. This can be accomplished with a light mixture of water and household bleach or B-Brite™. At the risk of sounding tiresome, DIRTY EQUIPMENT CAN CREATE BACTERIAL AND FUNGAL PROBLEMS THAT WILL RUIN YOUR BREW. Keep your equipment clean and you shouldn't have any major problems.

You should also prepare to have some clean, cold water. Many home brewers like to keep 3 to 5 gallons in the fridge at all times or you can just turn on the cold water faucet. Water, as you can see, is one of the key ingredients in brewing – it comprises about 90 percent of the liquid you will work with to make your brew. The quality of the water will help in determining how good the beer will be.

If you have a municipally supplied water, there is a tendency to over-chlorinate it and you may want to either boil it or run it through a countertop water filter. Both methods will help to reduce the chlorine content and ensure a better brew. Don't skimp on your water. If it entails having to buy spring or well water, then do it! As we all know from the legendary national beer advertisements (Coors and Rolling Rock in particular), they all stress the water source they use. In general, though, if you drink it on a daily basis, then your water source is good enough to use for your home brew.

Pour your clean cold water (through a sanitized funnel if you're a carboy user) into the fermentation vessel and then slowly add the malt and water mixture into the fermenter in similar fashion. After you have added all the mixture, seal the top of the fermenter with a lid (bucket) or a sanitized rubber plug (carboy). Pick up the fermenter and shake the cold and hot mixture to mix them well. If your mixture does not reach the 5 gallon level, add enough water to do so and mix well again.

If you are using other ingredients such as hops in your brew, make sure that you strain them before adding them to the fermenter. This will ensure that you have no particulate matter in the brew.

There is one more thing you should check before adding the yeast to your mixture. Using your hydrometer, check the specific gravity/density of the liquid. The hydrometer will let you know what the potential alcohol content will be of your brew and will also give you an indication of when to bottle it (more on this later).

*hydrometer*

Once you have mixed your hot and cold liquids well, aerate the wort well by stirring vigorously with a sanitized spoon and take a temperature reading. When the temperature drops below 78°F, you may add the yeast. There are optimum temperatures for the fermentation process. Most yeast strains seem to perform best between 70°F and 78°F and the resulting brew is benefited from a slow fermentation. A hot fermentation can yield flavor and aroma components that are not desirable in beer.

A California winemaker gave me a very basic education about yeast fermentation many years ago. He explained it by saying that yeast are very hungry little guys that just love to eat sugar and convert it into alcohol. They will continue to eat until they have converted all the sugar into alcohol and then they just die from overeating. It's a very basic explanation but it cuts right through all the chemical, biologicaland scientific data. If there is too much sugar, not enough sugar, too hot or too cold a fermentation, an incorrect yeast strain or other problems, fermentation may shut down because the environment is not quite right for these quixotic little fellows. To ensure good fermentation, consult the directions that accompany your malt extract package or your recipe – and take frequent hydrometer readings.

Well, what is a hydrometer you may ask? A good question because it is an essential piece of equipment. A hydrometer is an instrument that is used to measure the *specific gravity* or density of a liquid. If you add something like sugar to water,

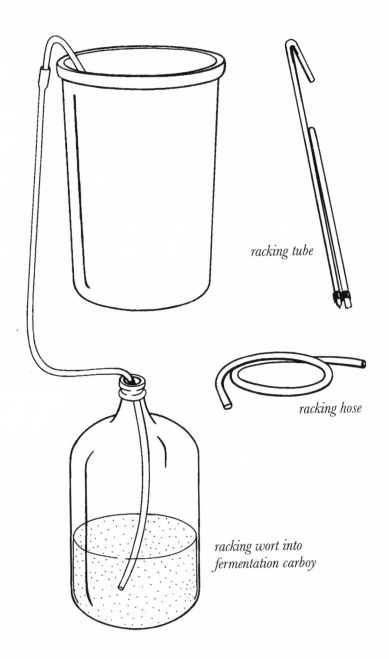

racking tube

racking hose

racking wort into
fermentation carboy

*HOME BREW*

the water becomes denser and the specific gravity rises upwards from 1.000, the density that has been assigned to water without any additions. Therefore, you can see that the density of the water will change because you have added malt extract or other adjuncts to the water.

Most hydrometers read most accurately at 60°F and home brewers must make adjustments to their calculations as the temperature in the liquid that is being measured rises or falls. Consult the instructions that come with your hydrometer to determine the optimal temperature for the one you own. With freshly created wort, you will need to take your sample and try to cool it to the proper temperature so that you get an ideal reading.

To get a good reading, fill the hydrometer vessel with wort up to the proper level, drop the hydrometer in the vessel and then read the scale. Remember to record the reading in the journal that you will keep of your brewing processes. After recording the reading, do not return this sample to the unfermented liquid! It could possibly contaminate the whole batch. Discard it or drink it (yes, drink it!) to understand what your wort tastes like.

Now that all the readings have been done and you feel comfortable with the temperature of the liquid – between 75°F and 80°F with 78°F being the ideal – then add (pitch, in brewing terms) your yeast to let the fermentation begin. Fermentation will later slow dramatically as the temperature decreases.

Carboy people, once the yeast has been added, attach a rubber stopper that will accommodate a blow-off hose or a fermentation lock. Bucket people, secure the lid firmly.

Depending on the size batch of beer you are making and

the size of your carboy, you may not need a blow-off hose. If the carboy holds about a gallon more of liquid than you are brewing, then you may simply affix the fermentation lock to the stopper. During the first two to three days you will see a great deal of fermentation action from the blow-off hose as the hungry yeast begin their job of converting the large amount of sugar to alcohol. You will certainly notice a fair amount of foaming.

Bucket users and nonhose carboy owners should use a fermentation lock. As usual, make sure it is very clean and sanitized before attaching it to the top of the carboy or the hole in the bucket lid. The fermentation lock allows fermentation gases to escape and keeps contamination out of the fermenting brew. The outpouring of the gases will not permit entrance of incoming harmful bacteria or fungi. The fermentation lock must be at least half full of water for it to function properly. During the first two to three days of fermentation you will notice a great deal of bubbling in the water. These are the gases escaping.

Once you see that fermentation is slowing or just about complete, you should again take hydrometer readings for a few days to confirm that you are correct in your assumption. Once you get the same readings two days in a row, then your fermentation is complete. Don't forget to clean the hydrometer well before use and don't pour the brew from the test back into the container (go on – drink it!).

When the fermentation is complete, you will note that there are particles that have precipitated to the bottom of the fermentation vessel. These are dead yeast cells which should be left behind when you bottle your brew. Do not disturb them because they may give undesirable flavors and aromas.

Invariably, you will have *some* sediment in your home brew – by and large this is not a problem, in fact some premier micros and imports contain small amounts of sediment. Just make it a point to minimize sediment whenever possible.

You will also see that there has been a perceptible color change in the brew from its conception. The brew will be of a darker hue and appear richer. Good job!

Time to bottle your first brew. Congratulations and don't get nervous. It's a simple task and if you get your spouse, significant other or a couple of friends, you can have a bottling party.

## BOTTLING YOUR BREW

As always, it is good to prepare in advance by organizing the area you'll be working in. Make sure you have plenty of room, that the area is clean and that you have access to water and priming material (see below). Just prior to bottling, you should clean and sanitize the following items: your bottles, your plastic bucket and your 6-foot length of hose. Also, you should boil your bottlecaps for about 5 or 6 minutes to sanitize them. Let them stand in the water after boiling until ready to use.

The priming liquid will be used to cause the secondary fermentation to take place in the bottle. This liquid is comprised of corn sugar or dried malt extract, mixed with water and then boiled for 5 minutes or so. The priming liquid will be mixed into your flat brew and the residual yeasts will begin the secondary fermentation. Those hungry little guys never want to give up!

When sanitizing the bucket and the bottles, you should mix about 5 gallons of cold water to about 2 ounces of bleach.

Place the bottles in a large clean tub or pail and add the sanitizing liquid. After sanitizing you must rinse the bottles. If you have purchased a bottle rinser, which is an excellent investment and will conserve water as well, hook it up to the faucet and rinse the bottles well with hot water. Sanitize your pail and the plastic hose with the same solution or make up a new batch for them. Rinse them well with hot water to ensure a great brew.

When making the priming liquid, add ¾ cups of corn sugar or 1¼ cups of dried malt extract with 16 ounces (1 pint) of water. Following years of experimenting and calculations by multitudes of home brewers, this is about perfect for making a great beer. Too much sugar will result in too much carbonation and will create the right environment for exploding beer bottles. What a wonderful mess this is to clean up! In days of yore, the practice of adding a priming agent was accomplished by adding sugar to each individual bottle – the problem was that each bottle would be a little different. By mixing the priming liquid into the whole batch of brew you achieve a very consistent brew from bottle to bottle.

After you have completed all of your tasks to get organized, it is time to bottle.

As a last precaution, take a final hydrometer reading to make sure you're on track. Remember that you will never achieve a specific gravity of water (1.000) because there will always be suspended solids in your liquid. You will probably get a reading of 1.004 to 1.019. If all is OK, proceed by placing the fermentation vessel in an elevated position – on a counter or a table. Pour the priming liquid into the sanitized bucket. Remove the plug from your carboy or lid from your bucket.

To insure that you have a proper siphon in the making, fill the hose with cold water to create a vacuum, and get a coworker to aid you by using the clamps that are widely available for this function. Place your end in the fermenting vessel while your friend lets the remaining water run into a waiting container. (There is an alternative to having an assistant: a racking tube that has a clamp attachment, which really simplifies the job.) If all is well, beer should follow right behind the water. As the beer begins to flow, move the end of the hose into the sanitized bucket so that it may be ready to accept the brew.

Keep the hose deep in the fermention vessel but above the sediment line where the dead yeast cells are lying. As the liquid moves (slowly and without much splashing into the container, please) relax and enjoy the experience. To moderate the flow of the liquid, pinch the hose with your fingers or the clamp to slow it down. Take it slowly. Once you have finished you can take the primed brew and place it on the counter or table and set up your bottling line.

Have your bottle capper, caps and bottles ready. Once again, make sure everything is clean and sanitized. A bottle filler specially designed for this task really simplifies the process. It fills the bottles to the correct level and takes less time than the old method of siphoning. It also leaves the right head space. Have your coworker assist with the capping so that you keep the bottles open for as short a time as possible. If you are brewing more beers, which you surely will be, you might want to mark the bottles or the caps with some sort of abbreviation for the type of brew it is. After bottling, make sure to clean all the equipment and utensils you have used. Dry them well and store them until their next use.

Place your bottles of home brew in a dark and quiet place, standing upright. Now begins the waiting game. The temperature should ideally be around 65°F to 68°F. The secondary fermentation will take a week to two weeks. As the yeasts slowly create this carbonation, you will notice a sediment begin to form at the bottom of the bottle. Once again, the yeasts are beginning to die and are falling to the bottom. You will also notice a clarification process in the brew as this occurs. For the home brewer, this is always the most difficult time because he wants to taste that beer. Well, you'll just have to wait. Anticipation is good for you and your brew.

The final part of this process is the most rewarding. Drinking the beer! As you will see, there's that sediment to contend with, but if you pour slowly and carefully, you can leave most of it behind in the bottle. The dead yeasts cells won't harm you, but they could add a yeasty character to the brew and will make it murky.

## PROBLEM SOLVING

Problems will arise from time to time in any brewing procedure. When they do happen, the best advise is to relax, step back, take a few deep breaths and begin to analyze the problem. The natural reaction is to get upset, wring your hands and utter epithets that are completely unnecessary. Most of the problems you will encounter can be solved pretty simply and with a little time can improve the quality of your brewing. Worst case, you'll have a basement full of sour beer but a valuable education to show for it!

If you follow the guidelines set forth in this book or any other well-researched book on the subject, you should have few, if any, problems. As mentioned earlier, good record keeping of your recipes, procedures and readings will ensure minimal troublesome occurrences. The record keeping will be your guidepost to the answers in most situations.

Some of the problems you may encounter along the brewing route are listed below with the suggested ways to proceed in correcting them. Take notes as you begin your analysis and the problem solving – it will benefit you at some point in your brewing career.

*OVERLY CARBONATED BEER:* Typically, the main source of this problem is too much priming sugar in the secondary fermentation. Measure carefully and follow the instructions in the recipe. The other source for overcarbonation is a bacterial infection. Bacteria can cause a brew to start a late fermentation of ingredients in the brew other than the sugar. The root cause for bacterial infections is lack of cleanliness. More information on bacteria follows.

*STUCK FERMENTATIONS:* These sometimes appear due to a lack of sugar in the primary or secondary fermentation, too high or low a temperature or the improper yeast for the type or style of beer being made. Another possibility is that the brew you are making will stop fermenting with a small amount of unfermented sugar still remaining. The small amount of residual sugar adds complexity and will be rounded out by the carbonation of the beer. The best thing to do is to bottle the beer and appreciate the richness of this style. There are specific yeast strains designed to ferment only certain amounts of sugar, while others that will ferment "bone dry." Therefore, you may not have a stuck fermentation at all.

*LACK OF CARBONATION:* If you have followed your recipe properly, this should not happen. Check your notes – maybe you stored the beer for the secondary fermentation in too cool a place, forgot to add the correct amount of sugar or have a yeast problem. Not to worry. Try moving the brew into a warmer environment to see if that helps. Uncap the bottles and add a few grains of yeast as a last-ditch effort – then recap. If all this fails, you have two options – throw the batch out or blend the flat batch with a well-made brew and you will have a reasonably nice beer to drink.

*SOUR AROMAS AND FLAVORS:* You haven't been very clean in your procedures or in your brewing process and now you have a bacterial infection. There is little you can do for it. The cause for this, besides contamination, is too warm an environment or too slow a fermentation process. Keep it clean and you will have better beer.

*CLOUDINESS:* Have the sediments from the fermentation been stirred up? If not, if you have a permanently hazy or cloudy look, it could be the result of another type of bacterial infection. Or it could be that you have used a less than fresh yeast for your fermentation. Try to use your yeasts when they are freshest.

A cloudy appearance may also be due to a "chill haze." This occurs in most home brews because they are not filtered to remove remaining tannins. If you refrigerate your beer and then remove it from the fridge, you will probably see a chill haze. But if you leave that same brew at room temperature until it warms up, you will see the chill haze disappear. In any event, chill hazed beer still tastes great and *you* are the one who made it.

*MOLDY BREW:* Once again, you have not been clean and sanitary in your brewery. Luckily, beer will not allow any *harmful* mold to exist, so you shouldn't get sick – but your beer may have off flavors. The best way to avoid this is to keep it clean and to not allow the brew to come into contact with bacteria or other harmful micro-organisms.

*BACTERIAL PROBLEMS:* As you see, most of the above situations have come about due to the infection of your beloved brew by bacteria. They can easily contaminate any and all surfaces of your brewery, infesting bottles, carboys, siphon hoses, malts, grains, wort and on and on. There are many beneficial bacteria that can make wonderful things like yogurt, but we don't want any bacteria near the brewery. Keep it clean!

A sure-fire sign that you have a bacteria problem is a narrow ring around the neck of the bottle at the level of the beer. If you have not cleaned your bottles and sanitized them properly, you are asking for instant contamination.

Following are some guidelines to help you avoid bacterial contamination. This list is basically a recap of the beginning of this chapter, but it is worth repeating these tips to prevent problems.

1) Check your fermenters, siphon hoses, air locks and other plastic items before using them. If you see stains or scratches, replace them. These areas are ideal spots for bacteria to grow. Use only food-grade plastic of the best quality.

2) After each brewing stage, make sure that all equipment is cleaned, and that all work surfaces and containers are clean and ready for the sanitizing process.

3) Install your fermentation lock properly and make sure that it has water in it; otherwise you will have problems.

4) When creating a siphon to transfer your brew from vessel to vessel, do not suck on the end as they did in days past. Rather, fill the hose with clean water to create the needed vacuum.

5) Cool your wort and aerate (stir) it well to allow for a good and complete fermentation. Do not stir it with your hands or a wooden spoon. Both have the porosity to harbor bacteria. Also, please don't cool your wort by adding ice to it.

6) Later, when you are siphoning your brew, try not to splash it—at this stage you *don't* want to aerate it. Be gentle when siphoning—there is no hurry.

7) Before bottling, soak your bottles in a bleach and water solution overnight to remove any stains or bacteria. Rinse the bottles well with hot water.

And finally, use lots of common sense at every step of the way. Think—could *this* be a potential area for the development of bacteria?

## THE ADVENT OF U-BREWS

So you don't want to go through all the hassles of buying equipment and ingredients, finding an area to work in your small apartment or house and yet you still want to brew a home style brew. Well, there may be a place where you can brew your beer outside of your house at almost the same cost as doing it at home. Slowly but surely, U-Brews, as they are known, are beginning to pop up throughout the United States. They are already well ensconced in Canada. Most of the American U-Brews are located west of the Mississippi, but one has recently opened in Philadelphia.

These operations have the newest and best equipment

available, offer the brewer the option of many styles and types of brew and there is the pleasure of creating a brew without the minor inconveniences of the true home brew.

On-premise brewing operations, as they are known in Canada, came about due to the extremely high taxes levied against beer purchased through the local government-owned stores. Many Canadians wishing to drink beer can't afford to do so and they have been forced to brew their own. In the United States, U-Brews or "personal micro-breweries" are popular among urban dwellers with little room to brew but plenty of thirst for fine beer.

The process for brewing at a U-Brew is virtually the same as working at home except you are working with the best equipment available on the market. The equipment is what a small micro-brewery would use – stainless steel kettles for boiling the wort; high-speed wort chillers; seven-step filtration systems; large, temperature-controlled boxes for the fermentation process (65°F); a carbonation system; counterpressure bottling system; custom label creator, and a computer data base of recipes and information.

The U-Brew in Philadelphia is operated by two young men who graduated from the University of Pennsylvania. They became interested in home brewing and realized that there was a call for a facility in the metro Philadelphia area. The location is close to all major highways and bridges leading to the city so that customers have easy access. The space itself is pristine and attended to constantly to keep all equipment clean and the environment as bacteria-free as possible. They feel that their customer base is predominately people looking to learn about home brewing and that a U-Brew is the simplest and most cost effective way to try brewing.

As a novice brewer, U-Brews walk you through the whole works for at least the first two times you brew so that you understand the process. They will help you select your recipe, organize the ingredients, give you a simple set of instructions and monitor your progress from the boiling of the wort to the pitching of the yeast. After you have pitched the yeast, the fermenter is rolled into the fermenting room where you leave it for two weeks. The staff monitors the progress, tasting and checking the brew. Then you come back and bottle your brew. The staff suggests that you buy the bottles necessary to bottle your brew and they will sterilize them thereafter for your subsequent beers.

Having seen some of their recipes, the U-Brews are relying on malt extracts predominately though some of their recipes do call for the addition of grains. Currently Philadelphia's America U-Brew is not doing all-grain brewing due to the time involved. They feel that most of their customers have not reached the level of education nor do they want to make the investment of all-grain brewing.

U-Brews have the potential to educate and introduce a broad spectrum of the general public to the joys and pleasures of home brewing. One hopes this is a fad that will turn into viable businesses that spread throughout the country.

# 4
# MALTS AND GRAINS

$A$s most of us know, fruit, be it grapes, berries or apples, is the source for the production of wine. With beer, we have learned that grains and their by-product malt, create the flavors and aromatics we love. This chapter will attempt to educate the reader about the malting process, the grains that are used and the basics in the art of all-grain brewing.

## THE MALTING PROCESS

Malting is a process that involves germinating (i.e., sprouting) grains and then drying them a special way to create the desired beer. The germination process would usually take place in the field naturally. What the maltster does is harvest the grains, soak them in water for a couple of days, then place them in a special area to provide the proper environment for germination. They are raked regularly and then are dried to preserve their freshness and to ensure the grains are separated.

Technology has aided the brewer and the maltster over

the centuries but many people feel that the traditional method of germination and drying is still the best. This method includes a long building specially constructed for this purpose with good ventilation and a stone or concrete flooring. The germinated grains are laid out in a thin layer the length of the flooring. The raking takes place by hand and the drying is accomplished over a fire with the grains sitting on a very fine, sieved flooring. Each country had its favorite type of wood or heat source that gave the malt its individual characteristics. Consider that Scotch whiskey is made from malted grains that have dried on peat harvested straight from the peat bogs – its aromatic and flavor components are due largely to this drying process.

Today, the malting process is completed in essentially the same manner with the addition of high-tech equipment that enables the maltster to be efficient and consistent from batch to batch. The grains are still soaked for two to three days to allow them to become water soluble and to release specific enzymes that will be needed in the fermentation as well as the mashing process. Once the grains have reached the ideal stage, they are spread in a thin layer on the germination floor and the raking procedure begins. This is accomplished in containers that are specifically built for this purpose. The grains are turned by rakes that are suspended from the ceiling or they are raked by automated tractors or spiral-like augers within the floor system. Air is also being fed into the system to aid in the germination process. This very moist air plus the raking allows the grain to germinate at an even pace throughout the container.

After the raking has been completed and the green malt has reached the proper germination stage and all the grains are separate from one another, then the drying must begin. Technology has replaced the wood fire. Today the grains are dried over heated air – this reduces the smoke factor of an open fire. The result is a more consistent malting that retains the components and quality the brewer is looking for to craft a great beer. What is missing from the current process is a slightly smoky character that lent some interesting and rich flavors to the beer of yore.

The green malt is placed into specifically designed kilns that allow for a slow, even drying and moisture reduction. This is typically done in two stages, a first heating at about 120°F for up to 18 hours to bring the moisture content to about 12 percent and a second heating at about 150°F for about 12 hours. The malt will also see a finishing for a few hours at 180°F to bring the moisture content down to the ideal of 4½ percent. The final procedure before the malt is sent out from the processor is a thorough inspection and the removal of any rootlets that might remain.

The length of time and the amount of heat that is used have a great affect on the style of beer being produced. As the duration of time and the temperature are increased, the grains will take on a darker and more caramelized look and flavor. This occurs because the sugars are essentially being cooked to a caramel. This adds complexity, richness, color and sometimes a perceived sweetness to the resulting beer.

The home brewer searching for a particular style of beer or ale may want to combine malts that have been treated to different drying/kilning procedures. The brewer looking for complexity may add a gently-kilned grain, suitable for a pilsener, to a grain that was dried at a higher temperature, used for darker ales. By doing this, the brewer begins to develop, through experimentation, a style or type of beer that will satisfy the palate and utilize the best of what the maltster has to offer.

To aid brewers worldwide, a scale has been developed to distinguish the types of malt available. This scale, known as Lovibond, was developed by the European Brewing Convention. The E.B.C. scale assigns certain numbers as the malt becomes darker. Malts suited for pilsener style will have numbers below 10, darker amber malts in multiples of 10s and malts suited for stouts and porter styles will be in the 100s.

Malt extract is a product that is attractive to brewers because of its lower cost and its convenience. Malt extracts come in all styles and with the addition of some whole-grain malt, they can make spectacular home brews. Even using an all-extract wort, one can make very fine beer.

Malt extracts are created using the same malt as whole-malt products. After the malt has finished at the maltsters, it is sent to a malt extract producer where it is ground and turned into grist and then it is mashed in large quantities. Although the quantities are huge, the process is very much the same as the one an all-grain brewer would use.

The malt is heated with water for specific amounts of time that allow the starches to change into fermentable sugars, which becomes the mash. Once this has been finished, the wort is drawn through a lauter tun.

For malt extract, the wort is recycled through the mash once or twice until it runs clear and then it is pasteurized to protect against molds or wild yeasts. Once this has been completed, the wort is sent through a reduction process that removes all but 20 percent of the water and reduces the remaining 80 percent to sugar solids. This is accomplished through a vacuum process that boils the wort at lower temperatures so that no problems arise due to over-caramelization of sugars from rapid boiling.

## THE GRAINS

For the home and commercial brewer the choice of useful grains is as varied as the variety of grapes for the home winemaker. The winemaker can use different types of fruits as well as grapes. The brewer has the same option, but it is a bit more limited. This section will review the grains that are available and the styles of beer that can be produced from them.

Barley, oats, rye, wheat, rice and corn are the most widely

*6-row barley*

used grains for brewing. Rye is the least used and corn and rice are the most widely used in the United States due to their availability and low cost. The quality of the grains and their malting process will make the difference in the brew. Rye will give the brew a hint of spice and herbs; barley gives sweet, clean flavors, wheat will put forth a tart, citric quality; and rice and corn have lighter and more delicate flavors.

Of all of these, barley is the most widely used for quality brewing. Upwards of 30 percent of all barley is used for malting of some type. There are many different types of barley used, whether they be "2-row" or "6-row" with variations thereof. Barley is thought to be the oldest of the cultivated grains. Some brewers prefer barleys that are planted in the spring, others prefer barleys planted in the winter months. Each type has its proponents and the barleys do have their individual characteristics. Barleys are grown all over the world and specific varieties are suited to specific climatic zones. Because it is planted in the winter and spring months, barley is a welcome crop – it can be rotated with other crops. Barley also uses the water of the winter and spring months very efficiently and is quite tolerant of salty soil.

Most farmers who produce barleys have opted for the higher yielding 6-row varieties and hence most brewers are compelled to use what is readily available. Six-row varieties are grown in the United States in the Northwest and Midwest.

Over the past twenty-five to thirty years, due to advancements in agricultural techniques and knowledge of soils and climatic influences, 2-row barleys are seeing more use by the farming community. This allows the brewer to find a variety of 2-row types at more affordable prices and to add more diversity to his beer styles. Two-row barleys have been more suited to northern climates – they are grown in the Northwest, Canada and Northern Europe – and brewers in these areas traditionally used them to produce their distinctive brews. The main differences between 2- and 6-row barley for the home brewer is that 2-row varieties will give the all-grain brewer a better extract and the 6-row types will work a bit better with added ingredients. Also, 6-row barley seems to give off more tannin flavors whereas 2-row barleys have a cleaner and softer taste on the palate.

There are two different types of malt as well – crystal and roasted. Crystal malts are treated by a special technique after they have been steeped and germinated in the usual fashion. The next step is the stewing, which is what maltsters call the crystal malt process. When the green malt is ready, it is placed in a special kiln where no moisture is permitted to escape and the temperature is raised to a mashing level of about 150°F. The husks begin to develop a ball of malt sugar. The kiln is then opened, the temperature is raised and the malt sugar begins to caramelize and darken as does the husk. The best known and respected of the crystal malts is Cara-Pils/ Dextrine. It adds a lovely, smooth and sweet quality to the brews it graces.

Roasted malts are made by the conventional method discussed earlier. Please remember that time and temperature in the kilning process will determine the flavors and colors of the roasted malts.

It is worth noting that many malts, worts and beers will carry a Lovibond rating to determine the color from light (1.5 L) to dark (530 L). Also there is a new method of determining color which is somewhat similar to Lovibond. That method, the Standard Reference Method (S.R.M.), is almost equivalent to Lovibond but actually gives a better reading of the color. For example, pilsener would have an S.R.M. of about 4 degrees and a color of yellow gold whereas a stout would have an S.R.M. around 35 to 40 degrees and a color of dark brown to black.

Barley in its malted form is widely available to the home brewer. It is sold in cans as malted extract or in its natural state as grain malts. The variety is outstanding and has allowed the amateur to produce excellent brews of all types and styles. For those brewers who want to use a malt extract and enhance the quality, the addition of grain malts to the boiling process will certainly reward you.

Following is a short list of malt extracts available to the home brewer. Included in each manufacturer's category will be an even briefer listing of styles they produce. Not all of these may be sold in your market, but always ask – you may be able to special order. Please note that all of these products include yeast and are hopped unless otherwise noted.

*Brewferm* from Belgium: abbey to oud bruin,
    also a kreik (cherry).
*Brewmaker* from England: I.P.A. to stout.
*Cooper* from Australia: lager to stout.
*Edme* from England: pilsener lager to supbru dark
    (also a wheat).
*Geordie* from England: lager, Scottish export,
    Yorkshire bitter.
*Ireks-Arkady* from Germany: Munich light, amber and
    weizen.

*Ironmaster* from England: European pale pilsener to northern brown ale.

*John Bull* from England: broad range from bitters to stout (also a barley wine).

*Laaglander* from Holland: light beer to Irish stout (also a traditional strong ale).

*Mountmellic* from Ireland: light lager to Irish stout.

*Munton and Fison* from England: one of the oldest and best producers; broad range from traditional bitter to export stout.

*Premier* from U.S.A.: lager, wheat and rice; unhopped.

*Red Bank* from U.S.A.: light, amber and dark.

Following is a short list of available grain malts for those wishing to improve their extract brews or wishing to produce all-grain beers.

*barley flakes*
*black patent malt*
*Cara-Pils / Dextrin malt*
*chocolate malt*
*crushed pale malt*
*crystal malt*
*Klages 2-Row*
*lager malt*
*roasted barley*
*Victory malt*
*Vienna malt*
*wheat malt*

A good home brew shop will be able to aid and direct you as to which malt will be best suited for the style of brew you wish to create. They will also have a malt mill to ensure that your malt is in ideal condition for the brewing of a great beer.

Briefly, here are a few words on some of the better known roasted malts.

*Barley flakes* are made from the best dehusked barleys that are cooked and flaked. They will typically produce a dry, mild-flavored, light-colored beer.

*Black patent or black malt* is roasted even hotter than chocolate malt and has a slightly burnt flavor profile. It also provides color and a sharp, acrid character that is typical of porters and stouts.

*Cara-Pils* is used for light to dark ales and adds body and foam retention.

*Chocolate malt* is known for its smooth flavor and is recommended for very fine dark ales. It is commonly used for color adjustment and will lend a chocolatelike flavor to the final brew.

*Roasted barley* is a misnomer because it is really not roasted and kilned in the same manner as other malts. It is roasted raw and has a coffeelike, sweet, burnt and grainy flavor profile. It contributes a red to deep brown color component.

*Victory malt* usually contributes a toasted and warm flavor profile and works nicely for ales from nut brown to amber to dark to porter.

*Vienna malt* makes a fine basic malt for a brew. Flavor profile offers a grainy and malty characteristic and a deep golden color. Ideal for everything from pilseners to ambers.

*Wheat malts* are used for the production of wheat beers. Malted wheat adds flavor components that are not obtainable from raw wheat.

The two main varieties of *oats* are the white and red. Home brewers will find that oats can be tricky and are mostly unnecessary. They have one of the highest protein counts of all the grains and high fat and oil content. These traits can cause difficulties in beer making.

Oats are used predominately to enhance the flavor and body of stouts. When used, you do not need a large quantity of oats to derive their benefits. A good supplier of home brewing ingredients will offer a few choices of oats for the intermediate and advanced brewer.

*Rye* is a grain that has traditionally been used for making whiskey and is used by some amateur and professional beer makers. Rye lends a dry, bitter, sometimes fruity characteristic to beer. Like oats, rye is one of the more difficult grains to brew with, due to its starchy qualities and ability to absorb water. This can create clogging problems in all-grain brewing.

*Wheat* as an addition to barley makes some of the most refreshing brews. Wheat can be difficult for the home all-grain brewer due to the fact that it is huskless and, like rye, will clog filters and siphons.

Wheat adds a distinctive clove, bananalike, citrus and spice character and crisp delicate flavors. Brewers add wheat to their barley mash to ensure head retention and to impart these desirable flavors. Originally a mainstay in Germany where both barley and wheat flourish, wheat beers are now being produced everywhere beer is made – even Seattle, home of Redhook's Wheat Hook Wheaten beer.

Since it adds relatively little complexity, *rice* as a brewing adjunct is used more on the commercial level than the home brew level. Rice has been cultivated as a food source for more than 4,000 years and has been used in brewing for almost as long. Rice gives beer a crisp, clean and light flavor and is cheap and readily available. Rice, for use in home brew, needs to be cooked slightly to allow for the proper fermentation to take place.

There are scores of other adjuncts that are available for the home brewer, including tapioca, millet (sorghum), buckwheat, Triticale™, quinoa and wild rice, not to mention honey, liquid smoke, chili peppers and orange peels! As you read up on brewing and home brew recipes, you might be amazed by the ponderous range of combinations and ingredients your brewing friends have cooked up. The best suggestion, for starters anyway, is to stick with what has made you and generations of others successful – malt, barley, wheat, and maybe oats and rye. As your proficiency increases, you might want to branch out. But you may have as much fun experimenting with these five and never thirst for a brew made from tapioca!

# 5
# HOPS AND YEASTS

*W*here would brewing be without the addition of that hoppy character that we all love so well? Hops seem to have come into wide use by European brewers about 200 years ago after it was discovered that they offered protection from spoilage. Prior to this, the brewer used herbs and spices to preserve and flavor his brews.

Hops, due to their resinlike, acidic and tannic qualities, are wonderful in aiding and preserving quality while adding an herbal, floral and bitter taste and aroma to beers. The addition of hops also helps the brewer by aiding in clarification and head retention; it cleanses the drinker's palate, retards bacteria growth and also coagulates and rids the beer of unwanted malt proteins.

Hops are a member of the nettle family and are first cousins of the cannabis plant. Some people claim there is a distinct aromatic quality that you get both from the dried hop and the cannabis plants. The cones/flowers of the female hop vine are what the brewer uses.

Two families of hops exist, but the only cultivated one is

the perennial *Humulus lupulus*. There are distinct varieties that are suited to each climatic and agricultural zone and there is a definite difference to each of these varieties.

Hops are grown throughout the world with major areas of production being England, Germany, Belgium, Australia, New Zealand, Japan, and the Pacific Northwest of the United States (Washington, Oregon and Idaho). The United States is now second to Germany in hop production with Washington State being the leading producer. Hops are a major agricultural industry due to heavy demand from the commercial brewing business.

Hops, as with grape vines, were first discovered in their wild form and over the years we have domesticated them. We have also tried to improve the quality and quantity of production. Many of the best and most respected hops were created by man using hybridization, mutation or mass selection methods.

Quality hops bring something very special both to the brewer and also to the grower and that is why they have been developed and have become widely respected and available. The grower is looking for production, disease and insect resistance and harvesting qualities for greater profitability; the brewer is looking for bittering compounds (alpha and beta acids) and aroma components (essential oils).

Because hops are an agricultural product, they are affected year to year by different rainfall amounts, soil conditions, sun exposure during the growing season and other environmental influences. Therefore, just like grapes, some years are better than others for production, quantity and quality of hops. Acids and essential oils will vary and you should keep this in mind when buying hops. Also, hops in their whole form can change if they become old or stale. Avoid them if you don't feel the quality is up to your standards.

The home brewer, luckily, has access to all of the commercially available types. Hops are now sold in six forms: loose, pelletized, plugs, hop extract, hop oil and compressed whole hops.

Now you understand hops are wonderful and crucial for fine beer making. So when and how are they used?

Hops, as we discussed above, are used to preserve beer, to aid in the brewing process and to add bitter, aromatic and other flavor components. Without hops, beer would tend to be somewhat flabby on the palate – the aromas would not be as interesting without the wonderful floral, citrus and tangy notes that are imparted by hops.

You can put hops into the wort at any time during the initial stages of the brewing process. Brewers may add hops at the initial boil, in the middle or at the end. The most important thing to know is timing – "bittering" or "boiling" hops must be boiled for 20 to 90 minutes; "aroma" or "finishing" hops normally go in for just a few minutes at the end of the boil. Read your recipe carefully to get the most out of your hops.

The amount of bitterness will differ with each style of beer and also with each variety of hop used. As you will see down the road, you regulate the amount of bitterness and hop character by your selection of hops and by timing the introduction of the hops.

To determine the amount of bitterness in beer, a scale has been developed to calculate and measure this factor – International Bitterness Units (I.B.U.s). Be aware that the amount of I.B.U.s in each style of beer may give a different impression on the palate. Certainly if a pilsener has 25 I.B.U.s and a stout has the same, the stout will taste decidedly less bitter because of its richness and complexity.

The other method of bitterness measurement used is called the Homebrew Bitterness Units (H.B.U.). It is actually a simpler I.B.U. equation for the amateur:

*percentage of alpha acids x weight (ounces) of hops = H.B.U.s*

For example, if a recipe calls for 2.5 ounces of 6 percent Cascade hops that would be equal to 15 H.B.U.s. The beauty of this system is that you can determine the right amount of hops even if the hops you chose are of a different alpha acid content or if you wish to substitute another variety.

Example 1: The Cascade hops you bought actually come in at 5.5 percent alpha acids. Using the reverse equation:

15 H.B.U. divided by 5.5 = 2.75 ounces of hops needed for the above recipe (instead of 2.5 ounces).

Example 2: You want to substitute Clusters hops for the Cascades and the Clusters is 7.5 percent alpha acids.

15 H.B.U. divided by 7.5 = 2 ounces of hops needed for the above recipe.

Another method of calculating the amount of hops to use as been developed by Dave Line, author of *The Big Book of Brewing.* It is called the *Alpha Acid Units* system (A.A.U.). It works like this: one A.A.U. equals the amount of acid in 1 ounce of hops with an alpha acid content of 1 percent. In other words, if you buy ½ ounce of Goldings (alpha acid 5 percent) that would equal 2.5 A.A.U.'s.

For the home brewer, the variety of quality hops is very intriguing. Below is a short description of widely available hops, in plug, pellet or dried compressed whole hops. That will be followed by a chart listing the hop, alpha acids (percentage, which may vary) for fresh hops, country of origin and a comment or two. They will be listed first by bittering hops followed by aroma hops to make it easier to understand.

## BITTERING HOPS

*Brewers Gold:* Again, a dispute over the originating country. Slightly higher alpha content than Northern Brewer and a bit sweeter.

*Chinook:* Developed over the past 10 years in the United States, high alpha content and nice aromatics.

*Clusters:* Used as the standard bittering hop worldwide since the early 1900s. Thought to be a cross between a European and wild American hops. Its use is declining slightly.

*Galena:* Fast replacing Clusters as the most popular bittering hop. Developed in the United States. Very high alpha content.

*Northern Brewer:* Some argument as to the source – Germany, Britain or the United States. Good bittering qualities.

*Nugget:* A new variety with high alpha content. Very good bitterness quality.

*Perle:* Developed from Northern Brewer in Germany and now being produced in the Pacific Northwest. Good bittering profile.

Other bittering hops: *Banner, Bullion, Columbia, Comet, Pride of Ringwood, Talisman, Wye Target.*

# BITTERING HOPS

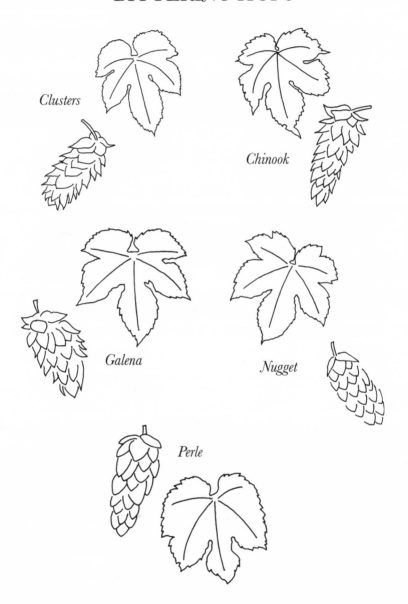

Clusters

Chinook

Galena

Nugget

Perle

# AROMA HOPS

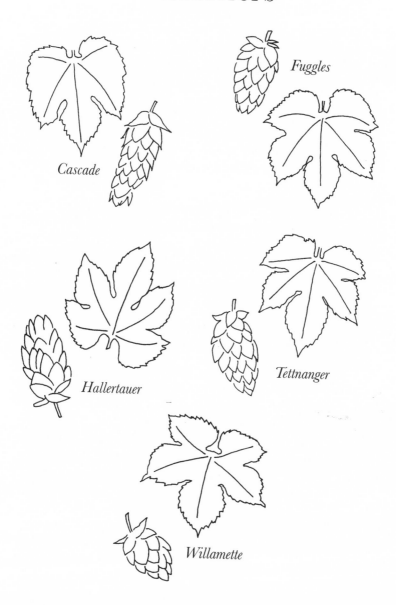

Cascade

Fuggles

Hallertauer

Tettnanger

Willamette

## AROMA HOPS

*Cascade:* Developed in the United States from a Fuggles seed. Has very good aromatics.

*Fuggles:* English variety developed around late 1800s. One reason Guinness has its distinct quality.

*Goldings:* Again, of English derivation and developed in the late 1700s. Kent Goldings are quite similar.

*Hallertauer:* Less used because of low yields, but still considered one of the best from Germany.

*Hersbrucker:* Another premium Germany variety with good aromatic profile.

*Mt. Hood:* New variety created in the United States from Hallertauer. Becoming popular due to its parentage and good alpha content and aroma.

*Saaz:* Developed in Czechoslovakia for the classic pilsener lagers of that region.

*Tettnanger:* Widely planted in the United States, but of German origin. Low yield and high quality.

*Willamette:* Recently developed in the United States and fast replacing Fuggles as the primary aroma hop.

Other aroma hops: *Spalt, Aquila, Styrian Goldings, Centennial.*

# HOP STATISTICS AND CHARACTERISTICS

| VARIETY | percentage of Alpha Acids | ORIGIN | COMMENTS |
|---|---|---|---|
| **BITTERING HOPS** | | | |
| *Chinook* | 11.0 | U.S.A. | Very good freshness and spicy aromas |
| *Clusters* | 7.0 | U.S.A. | Considered the best for aromas and a good bittering hop |
| *Galena* | 11.5 | U.S.A. | Neutral aromas if used early in the boil |
| *Northern Brewer* | 7.5 | U.S.A./ Germany | Robust and bitter |
| *Brewers Gold* | 8.5 | U.S.A./ Britain | Used as an ale hop, quite coarse tasting |
| *Nugget* | 12.0 | U.S.A. | Spicy and herbal aromas and good bittering |
| *Perle* | 8.5 | Germany | Nice aromas to go along with its bittering |
| *Banner* | 9.0 | U.S.A. | Brand new and quite good for bittering |
| *Bullion* | 9.5 | U.S.A./ Britain | Good all-around hop for bittering |

| VARIETY | percentage of Alpha Acids | ORIGIN | COMMENTS |
|---|---|---|---|
| *Columbia* | 9.5 | U.S.A. | Very rare and almost obsolete |
| *Comet* | 10.0 | U.S.A. | Same as above |
| *Pride of Ringwood* | 8.5 | Australia | Good bittering hop |
| *Talisman* | 8.5 | U.S.A. | Similar in style to Clusters; limited use |
| *Wye Target* | 10.5 | Britain | Not seen often; bitter, replacing Fuggles in U.K. |

AROMA HOPS

| | | | |
|---|---|---|---|
| *Willamette* | 5.0 | U.S.A. | Superb aromas for ales |
| *Fuggles* | 4.5 | Britain | Traditional ale hop |
| *Goldings* | 5.0 | Britain | Rich and earthy for ales |
| *Kent Goldings* | 5.0 | Britain | Same as above |
| *Hallertauer* | 4.5 | Germany | Wonderful spicy aromas; United States version different from German variety |
| *Hersbrucker* | 5.0 | Germany | Spicy and aromatic |

| VARIETY | percentage of Alpha Acids | ORIGIN | COMMENTS |
|---|---|---|---|
| *Saaz* | 5.0 | Czech. | Lager hop for pilsener noble spicy aromas |
| *Tettnanger* | 5.0 | U.S.A/ Germany | Finest hops in the world. United States: floral; German: spice-like aromas |
| *Cascade* | 5.5 | U.S.A | Citrus aromas and a good bittering hop, too |
| *Mt. Hood* | 5.5 | U.S.A. | Hallertauer quality and good alpha content |
| *Spalt* | 7.0 | Germany | Used as both bittering and aroma hop |
| *Aquila* | 7.0 | U.S.A. | Brand new aroma hop |
| *Styrian Goldings* | 6.0 | Yugoslavia/ U.S.Aand | Quite aromatic, good for ales |
| *Centennial* | 8.0 | U.S.A. | Hybrid of Cascade, very citrusy and aromatic |

# YEASTS AND THEIR CHARACTERISTICS

There are two different types of yeast about which the brewer should be knowledgeable: *Saccharomyces cerevisiae* and *Saccharomyces uvarum*. The two yeasts are very different in their functions for brewers, professional and amateur. The *cerevisiae* is used for top-fermenting ales and the *uvarum* is used for bottom fermenting lager/pilsener brews.

The *uvarum* were formerly known as *Carlsbergensis,* having been discovered in Denmark, and have become associated through the years with Bavarian-style lagers and pilseners.

The ale yeast will ferment at warmer temperatures and will have more complexity and depth of flavor. Ale yeasts have specific types within their family that have the potential to ferment from 55°F to 75°F. The lager/pilsener yeasts ferment typically at lower temperatures, 32°F to 55°F, and really stress the clean flavors and taste of the malts and hops utilized.

Although all ale yeasts, by nature, gather at the top of the fermenter to do their job, they will eventually precipitate to the bottom of the fermenter after completion. These ale yeasts, due to their warmer fermentations, give off an alelike character. Of course, flavor and aroma are also influenced by other ingredients.

Lager yeasts, on the other hand, will gather (flocculate) at the top of the fermenter initially and then settle at the bottom to complete the fermentation process. They like to ferment at around 45°F but they will also create nice brews at "room temperature" – around 65°F. Try to get as close to the low 50-degree range for the best results. Again, the resulting flavor and aroma profile will certainly depend on the strain of yeast and also the other ingredients used.

There are many different styles of both yeast strains available on the market. Most novice home brewers will use dried yeast in individual packages. These produce very fine brews if they are rehydrated properly so that they become active. The other popular type of yeast is packaged in liquid form. Liquid yeast has been proven to yield excellent results for most brewers who have the knowledge and willingness to work with it. Consult your local brew supply shop to determine which type will be best suited to your needs.

Each yeast is usually rated for its ability to metabolize the sugars in the wort. This "attenuation rating" is usually given in percentages with a range of about 4 percent. Attenuation rating is important because there are many different types of sugars in wort, and the brewer is looking for yeast that can ferment as many of them as possible to create a dry-tasting beer. At the same time, there are always brewers seeking a strain that will leave some unfermented sugars for a specialty beer. Again, talk to your brew supply retailer for specific information about the attenuation rating of the yeast you want to use.

# 6

# *HOME BREW RECIPES*

*T*his chapter will give you some very good recipes that have been developed by John Kleinschmidt of Brunswick Brewing Supply in Highland Park, New Jersey. All of these recipes have been tested and they should be quite easy to follow for beginning and advanced home brewers alike.

Recipes are given for malt-extract brewing as well as for all-grain brewing. You will notice that almost all of the malt-extract versions do contain a portion of specialty grains. Please consult your home brew supply for the necessary ingredients and other directions you may require. The recipes include notations for Homebrew Bitterness Units (HBU) for the suggested hops. Refer to the chapter on hops and yeasts for the conversion formula. Please note that for all-grain brewing you will need more equipment; consult the chapter on the home brewery and your local supply shop to determine the equipment and expertise you will need to make a given recipe.

At the end of this chapter you will find instructions for brewing beers according to the malt-extract method; please refer to this section when preparing to brew.

*All of the following recipes will brew about 5 gallons of beer.*

# THE ALES OF THE BRITISH ISLES

## *SESSION ALE*
### MALT-EXTRACT VERSION

Session ales are also known as bitters and are normally quite low in alcohol, about 3.2 percent to 3.5 percent. The term "session" arose because these ales can be consumed by groups of people during long "sessions" of business lunches or dinners. Because of their low alcohol level, they have a less adverse affect on the drinker's ability to function normally (at least in principle!). This session ale is normally blond to dark brown in color as a typical bitters would be.

*3 lbs light malt extract, liquid or dry*
*1½ lbs amber malt extract, preferably dry, but you can use liquid*
*1 lb British pale malt, whole grain*
*1 lb caramel malt, 60 Lovibond, whole grain*
*5 HBU Fuggles hops, for bittering/boiling*
*4 HBU Goldings hops, for finishing/aroma*
*1 package dried ale yeast*

## SESSION ALE
### ALL-GRAIN VERSION

*6 lbs British pale ale malt, whole grain*
*1 lb caramel malt, 40 Lovibond, whole grain*
*½ lb Cara-Pils malt, whole grain*
*5 HBU Fuggles hops, for bittering/boiling*
*4 HBU Goldings for finishing/aroma*
*1 package Wyeast London Ale Yeast, No. 1028*

## PALE ALE
### MALT-EXTRACT VERSION

Pale ales, as you will remember, have a touch of color leaning toward a light reddish hue and a bit of nuttiness on the palate.

*3 lbs light malt extract, liquid or dry*
*3 lbs amber malt extract, liquid or dry*
*1 lb British pale ale malt, whole grain*
*½ lb caramel malt, 40 Lovibond, whole grain*
*¼ lb Cara-Pils malt, whole grain*
*7 HBU Goldings hops for boiling/bittering*
*7 HBU Goldings hops for flavoring*
*4 HBU Fuggles hops for finishing/aroma*
*1 package dried ale yeast*

# PALE ALE
## ALL-GRAIN VERSION

*9 lbs British pale ale malt, whole grain*
*1½ lbs caramel malt, 40 Lovibond, whole grain*
*6 ounces Victory malt, whole grain*
*7 HBU Goldings hops for boiling/bittering*
*7 HBU Goldings hops for flavoring*
*4 HBU Fuggles hops for finishing/aroma*
*1 package Wyeast London Ale Yeast, No. 1028*

# INDIA PALE ALE, TRADITIONAL
## MALT-EXTRACT VERSION

As you can tell from the following recipe, I.P.A.s have a quite
hoppy character, light body and light to golden amber color.

*3 lbs light malt extract, liquid or dry*
*6 lbs amber malt extract, liquid or dry*
*1 lb caramel malt, 40 Lovibond, whole grain*
*½ lb wheat, whole grain*
*10 HBU Northern Brewer hops for bittering*
*5 HBU Goldings hops for flavoring*
*2 HBU Goldings hops for finishing/aroma*
*1 package Wyeast British Ale Yeast, No. 1098*

## INDIA PALE ALE, TRADITIONAL
### ALL-GRAIN VERSION

*12 lbs British pale ale malt, whole grain*
*1 lb caramel malt, 80 Lovibond, whole grain*
*1 lb Victory malt, whole grain*
*10 HBU Northern Brewer hops for bittering*
*5 HBU Goldings hops for flavoring*
*2 HBU Goldings hops for finishing*
*1 package Wyeast British Ale Yeast, No. 1098*

## BROWN ALE, NORTHERN
### MALT-EXTRACT VERSION

Developed in England, these brews are quite pleasureable to make and they possess a wonderful taste and color profile. They have a nice amber color and perhaps a touch of sweetness from the malts.

*3 lbs amber malt extract, liquid or dry*
*3 lbs dark malt extract, liquid or dry*
*1 lb caramel malt, 120 Lovibond, whole grain*
*1 lb Munich malt, whole grain*
*¼ lb chocolate malt, whole grain*
*6 ounces roasted barley, whole grain*
*9 HBU Bullion hops for bittering*
*3 HBU Fuggles hops for finishing*
*1 package dried ale yeast*

## BROWN ALE, NORTHERN
### ALL-GRAIN VERSION

*8 lbs British pale ale malt, whole grain*
*1 lb caramel malt, 120 Lovibond, whole grain*
*1 lb Munich malt, whole grain*
*½ lb chocolate malt, whole grain*
*½ lb roasted barley malt, whole grain*
*9 HBU Bullion hops for bittering*
*3 HBU Fuggles hops for finishing*
*1 package Wyeast British Ale Yeast, No. 1098*


## BROWN ALE, SOUTHERN
### MALT-EXTRACT VERSION

*3 lbs amber malt extract, liquid or dry*
*3 lbs dark malt extract, liquid or dry*
*1 lb caramel malt, 120 Lovibond, whole grain*
*1 lb Munich malt, whole grain*
*5 HBU Goldings hops for bittering*
*3 HBU Fuggles hops for finishing*
*1 package dried ale yeast*

## BROWN ALE, SOUTHERN
### ALL-GRAIN VERSION

*8 lbs British pale ale malt*
*1 lb caramel malt, 120 Lovibond*
*1 lb Munich malt*
*5 HBU Goldings hops for bittering*
*3 HBU Fuggles hops for finishing*
*1 package Wyeast British Yeast, No. 1098*


## PORTER-STYLE ALE
### MALT-EXTRACT VERSION

Due to the dark roasted malts, this brew has a caramel/coffee note and a wonderful deep color.

*6 lbs amber malt extract*
*1 lb dark malt extract*
*1 lb caramel malt, 80 Lovibond, whole grain*
*6 ounces chocolate malt, whole grain*
*1 ounce black malt, whole grain*
*8 HBU Northern Brewer hops for bittering*
*5 HBU Goldings hops for finishing*
*1 package of dried ale yeast*

## PORTER-STYLE ALE
### ALL-GRAIN VERSION

*10 lbs British pale ale malt*
*1 lb caramel malt, 80 Lovibond*
*6 ounces chocolate malt*
*3 ounces black malt*
*8 HBU Northern Brewer hops for bittering*
*5 HBU Goldings hops for finishing*
*1 package of Wyeast Irish Ale Yeast, No. 1084*


## STOUT-STYLE ALE
### MALT-EXTRACT VERSION

A classic stout will be quite rich with almost chocolate under-tones and a wonderful bittering quality from the hops. It is quite formidable considering how rich and sweet it could be if the proper hops were not used.

*3 lbs amber malt extract*
*3 lbs dark malt extract*
*1 lb flaked barley malt, whole grain*
*8 ounces roasted barley malt, whole grain*
*6 ounces chocolate malt, whole grain*
*2 ounces Black Patent malt, whole grain*
*9 HBU Northern Brewer hops for bittering*
*no finishing hops are necessary*
*1 package dried ale yeast*

# STOUT-STYLE ALE
## ALL-GRAIN VERSION

*8 lbs British pale ale malt*
*1 lb wheat grain*
*½ lb flaked barley malt*
*1 lb roasted barley malt*
*½ lb Victory malt*
*6 ounces chocolate malt*
*2 ounces Black Patent malt*
*9 HBU Brewers Gold hops to bitter (no finishing hops necessary)*
*1 package Wyeast British Ale, No. 1098*

# CONTINENTAL EUROPEAN BEERS

## BELGIAN-STYLE "SAISON"
### MALT-EXTRACT VERSION

Refreshing and crisp with a nice dash of hoppiness and spice from the finishing ingredients. A fine brew for the spring and summer months.

*6½ lbs light malt extract*
*2 ounces crystal malt, 20 Lovibond, whole grain*
*⅓ ounce chocolate malt, whole grain*
*½ lb wheat malt, whole grain*
*½ lb granulated sugar*
*3 HBU Hallertauer hops for bittering*
*2.4 HBU Saaz hops for finishing*
*⅓ ounce coriander seeds, cracked, for finishing*
*1 package Wyeast Belgian Ale Yeast, No. 1214*

## BELGIAN-STYLE "SAISON"
### ALL-GRAIN VERSION

*6 lbs pilsener malt*
*6 lbs pale ale malt*
*1 lb wheat malt*
*2 ounces crystal malt, 20 Lovibond*
*⅓ ounce chocolate malt*
*3 HBU Hallertauer hops for bittering*
*2.4 HBU Saaz hops for finishing*
*⅓ ounce coriander seeds, cracked, for finishing*
*1 package Wyeast Belgian Ale Yeast, No. 1214*

## BELGIAN-STYLE "DUBBLE" ALE
### MALT-EXTRACT VERSION

This classic Belgian was developed around the turn of the twentieth century as brewers realized the quality that could be achieved using the best techniques and ingredients.

*7 lbs light malt extract*
*2 lbs gold malt extract, liquid preferred*
*5 ounces caramel malt, 60 Lovibond, whole grain*
*¾ lb brown sugar*
*3 HBU Styrian Goldings hops for bittering*
*2.6 HBU Hallertauer hops for bittering*
*2 HBU Saaz hops for finishing*
*4 pieces orange zest, ⅛ x ½ inch, for finishing*
*1 package Wyeast Belgian Ale Yeast, No. 1214*

## BELGIAN-STYLE "DUBBLE" ALE
### ALL-GRAIN VERSION

*10 lbs pale malt*
*5 ounces caramel malt, 60 Lovibond*
*¾ lb brown sugar*
*3 HBU Styrian Goldings hops for bittering*
*2.6 HBU Hallertauer hops for bittering*
*2 HBU Saaz hops for finishing*
*4 pieces orange zest, ⅛ x ½ inch, for finishing*
*1 package Wyeast Belgian Ale Yeast, No. 1214*


## BELGIAN-STYLE "TRIPPEL" ALE
### MALT-EXTRACT VERSION

It is important to note that this ale must be almost as light in color as a pilsener to be true to its style. Select the lightest malt extract available.

*12 lbs light malt extract*
*½ lb Cara-Pils malt, whole grain*
*1½ lbs invert sugar (corn sugar)*
*3.2 HBU Hallertauer hops for bittering*
*3 HBU Goldings hops for bittering*
*2 HBU Saaz hops for finishing*
*1 package Wyeast Belgian Ale Yeast, No. 1214*

## BELGIAN-STYLE "TRIPPEL" ALE
### ALL-GRAIN VERSION

*12 lbs pilsener malt*
*2 lbs British pale ale malt*
*1 lb Cara-Pils malt*
*1½ lbs invert sugar*
*3.2 HBU Hallertauer hops for bittering*
*3 HBU Goldings hops for bittering*
*2 HBU Saaz hops for finishing*
*1 package Wyeast Belgian Ale Yeast, No. 1214*

## BELGIAN-STYLE "WHIT" ALE
### MALT-EXTRACT VERSION

This is a lighter style of Belgian with almost half wheat. The addition of the coriander really adds some interesting characteristics.

*4 lbs light malt extract*
*4 lbs wheat malt extract*
*3 HBU Saaz hops for bittering*
*3 HBU Saaz hops for finishing*
*1 oz coriander seeds, cracked, for finishing*
*1 package Wyeast Belgian White Yeast, No. 3944*

## BELGIAN-STYLE "WHIT" ALE
### ALL-GRAIN VERSION

*6 lbs pilsener malt*
*4 lbs wheat malt*
*3 HBU Saaz hops for bittering*
*3 HBU Saaz hops for finishing*
*1 oz coriander seeds, cracked for finishing*
*1 package Wyeast Belgian Whit Yeast, No. 3944*


## GERMAN-STYLE "HEFE WEIZEN" WHEAT BEER
### MALT-EXTRACT VERSION

Typically this brew has yeast at the bottom of the bottle so you may want to decant it slowly from the bottle to your glass.

*4 lbs light malt extract*
*4 lbs wheat malt extract*
*1 lb wheat, whole grain*
*1 lb pale ale malt, whole grain*
*2.4 HBU Hallertauer hops for bittering*
*4 HBU Tettnanger hops for finishing*
*1 package Wyeast Weihenstephan Yeast, No. 3068*

## GERMAN-STYLE "HEFE WEIZEN" WHEAT BEER
### ALL-GRAIN VERSION

*7 lbs pale ale malt*
*3 lbs wheat malt extract*
*3.4 HBU Hallertauer hops for bittering*
*4 HBU Tettnanger hops for finishing*
*1 package Wyeast Weihenstephan Yeast, No. 3068*


## GERMAN-STYLE "DUNKLE WEISS" BEER
### MALT-EXTRACT VERSION

This is a darker colored style of wheat beer that will show more of a malt profile than the previous recipe.

*5 lbs dark malt extract*
*4 lbs wheat malt extract*
*4 HBU Tettnanger hops for bittering*
*no hops are necesary for finishing*
*1 package Wyeast Weihenstephan Yeast, No. 3068*

## GERMAN-STYLE "DUNKLE WEISS" BEER
### ALL-GRAIN VERSION

*6 lbs pale malt*
*4 lbs wheat malt extract*
*1 lb special "B" malt*
*4 HBU Tettnanger hops for bittering*
*no finishing hops are necessary*
*1 package of Weihenstephan Yeast, No. 3068*

## GERMAN-STYLE "BOCK" BEER
### MALT-EXTRACT VERSION

Lots of richness here from the darker roasted malts, but also a nice bittering and middle mouth from the hops.

*4 lbs amber malt extract*
*4 lbs dark malt extract*
*1 lb Munich malt, whole grain*
*1 lb caramel malt, 120 Lovibond, whole grain*
*3 oz chocolate malt, whole grain*
*6.2 HBU Hallertauer hops for bittering*
*4 HBU Tettnanger hops for flavoring*
*no finishng hops are necessary*
*1 package dried lager yeast*
      *or*
*1 package Wyeast Munich Lager Yeast, No. 2308*

## GERMAN-STYLE "BOCK" BEER
### ALL-GRAIN VERSION

*2 lbs pilsener malt*
*10 lbs Munich malt*
*1 lb caramel malt, 120 Lovibond*
*3 oz chocolate malt*
*6.2 HBU Halleratuer hops for bittering*
*4 HBU Tettnanger hops for flavoring*
*no hops are necessary for finishing*
*1 package Wyeast Munich Lager Yeast, No. 2308*


## GERMAN-STYLE "MAIBOCK" BEER
### MALT-EXTRACT VERSION

Maibock is a slightly paler version of a bock and is traditionally associated with late spring (May). It does retain the malty characteristics of a bock even though the color is a bit lighter.

*7 lbs amber malt extract*
*2 lbs Munich malt, whole grain*
*1 lb caramel malt, 10 Lovibond, whole grain*
*4 HBU Northern Brewer hops for bittering*
*3.2 HBU Hallertauer hops for flavoring*
*4 HBU Tettnanger hops for finishing*
*1 package of dried lager yeast*

## GERMAN-STYLE "MAIBOCK" BEER
### ALL-GRAIN VERSION

*6 lbs pilsener malt*
*6 lbs Munich malt*
*1 ½ lbs caramel malt, 10 Lovibond*
*4 HBU Northern Brewer hops for bittering*
*3.2 HBU Hallertauer hops for flavoring*
*4 HBU Tttnanger hops for finishing*
*1 package Wyeast Bavarian Lager Yeast, No. 2206*


## GERMAN-STYLE PILSENER
### MALT-EXTRACT VERSION

It is important to note that if you are brewing the malt extract recipe, you should use the lightest color malt extract available.

*6 lbs light malt extract*
*1 lb Cara-Pils malt, whole grain*
*8 HBU Northern Brewer hops for bittering*
*3.2 HBU Hallertauer hops for finishing*
*1 package dried lager yeast*

## GERMAN-STYLE PILSENER
### ALL-GRAIN VERSION

*7½ lbs pilsener malt*
*1 lb Cara-Pils malt*
*8 HBU Northern Brewer hops for bittering*
*3.2 HBU Hallertauer hops for finishing*
*1 package Wyeast Pilsener Lager Yeast, No. 2007*

## CZECH PILSENER-STYLE BEER
### MALT-EXTRACT VERSION

For this brew in the malt extract version, you must use the lightest malt extract available to make a true-to-type beer. This is the classic pilsener and has wonderful flavors and flowery hoppy aromas.

*7 lbs light malt extract*
*½ lb Cara-Pils malt, whole grain*
*8 HBU Saaz hops for bittering*
*8 HBU Saaz hops for flavoring*
*8 HBU Saaz hops for finishing*
*1 package Wyeast Czech Pils Yeast, No. 2278*

# CZECH PILSENER-STYLE BEER
## ALL-GRAIN VERSION

*12 lbs pilsener malt*
*½ lb Cara-Pils malt*
*8 HBU Saaz hops for bittering*
*8 HBU Saaz hops for flavoring*
*8 HBU Saaz hops for finishing*
*1 package Wyeast Czech Pils Yeast, No. 2278*

# THE NEW GENERATION
# OF AMERICAN BEERS

## *NEW AMERICAN ALE, WESTERN STYLE*
### MALT-EXTRACT VERSION

*7 lbs amber malt extract*
*1 lb Munich malt, whole grain*
*½ lb caramel malt, 10 Lovibond, whole grain*
*½ lb wheat, whole grain*
*½ lb Cara-Pils, whole grain*
*9 HBU Cascade hops for bittering*
*4 HBU Tattnanger hops for flavoring*
*4 HBU Cascade hops for finishing*
*1 package dried ale yeast*


## *NEW AMERICAN ALE, WESTERN STYLE*
### ALL-GRAIN VERSION

*11 lbs 2-row malted barley*
*2 lbs caramel malt, 10 Lovibond*
*1 lb wheat*
*9 HBU Cascade hops for bittering*
*4 HBU Tettnanger hops for flavoring*
*4 HBU Cascade hops for finishing*
*1 package Wyeast American Ale Yeast, No. 1056*

## NEW AMERICAN LAGER, EAST COAST STYLE
### MALT-EXTRACT VERSION

*4 lbs light malt extract*
*3 lbs gold malt extract*
*½ lb Victory malt, whole grain*
*½ lb caramel malt, 40 Lovibond, whole grain*
*7.5 HBU Tettnanger hops for bittering*
*3.2 HBU Hallertauer hops for flavoring*
*4 HBU Willamette hops for finishing*
*1 package dried ale yeast*


## NEW AMERICAN LAGER, EAST COAST STYLE
### ALL-GRAIN VERSION

*12 lbs 6-row malted barley*
*1 lb  caramel malt, 40 Lovibond*
*7.5 HBU Tettnanger hops for bittering*
*3.2 HBU Hallertauer hops for bittering*
*4 HBU Northern Brewer hops for finishing*
*1 package Wyeast American Lager Yeast, No. 2035*

## AMERICAN-STYLE INDIA PALE ALE
### MALT-EXTRACT VERSION

*4 lbs amber malt extract*
*5 lbs light malt extract*
*1 lb Victory malt, whole grain*
*1 lb wheat, whole grain*
*11 HBU Eroica hops for bittering*
*8 HBU Brewers Gold hops for finishing*
*1 package dried ale yeast*


## AMERICAN-STYLE INDIA PALE ALE
### ALL-GRAIN VERSION

*12 lbs British pale ale malt*
*1 lb Victory malt*
*1 lb Cara-Pils malt*
*11 HBU Eroica hops for bittering*
*8 HBU Brewers Gold hops for finishing*
*1 package Wyeast American Ale Yeast, No. 1056*


The recipes in this chapter were chosen for their classic natures. There are, literally, thousands of recipes available to the home brewer, but we wanted to concentrate on the best and let you branch out from here. At the end of this book is a list of reference books for the home brewer. To expand your knowledge, please search out these other fine books to develop a more thorough grasp of the multiplicity of beer styles available to the home brewer.

# HOME BREWING UTILIZING THE RECIPES

Following are the basic guidelines that John Kleinschmidt suggests to all of his novice and intermediate home brewers. This procedure will allow you to make all of the malt extract recipes in this book.

There will not be a procedure given to make all-grain recipes because it could take up a whole book in itself. If you wish to make all-grain brews, it is highly recommended that you become fully knowlegeable about the advanced brewing techniques essential to this type of brewing. Most home brew shops will be able to guide you to a good book and to a group of people or an individual who could become your mentor. The quality differences between an all-grain and a malt-extract brew can be quite remarkable.

Good luck following the direcions below – they're really quite simple.

With malt extracts, your main function when you begin is to make the very viscous extract less viscous. The only logical way to accomplish this task is by warming the liquid. Extract usually comes packed in cans or a plastic bag. Either warm the container in a hot water bath or microwave the bag for a couple of minutes. Once this minor task has been completed, you can begin.

If your recipe contains whole/specialty grains (as most, if not all, of the recipes in this book do), then you must also have a steeping bag to contain them. Place the grains in the bag and then into a large soup pot that will be able to hold the bag plus enough water to entirely cover the bag. Place the bag and the cold tap water in the pot and turn on the burner. Allow the temperature to reach 155° F and let it remain there and steep the grains for one-half hour.

After one-half hour, remove the steeping bag from the liquid and let the remaining liquid drain out of the bag into the pot (use a colander). Do not squeeze the bag. Discard the steeping bag and the spent grains. Combine the liquid with the malt extract in a larger pot. The ideal size is one that will accommodate a minimum of 4 gallons. Make sure that the pot is *not* made of aluminum. Aluminum has a tendency to give beer an oxidative taste profile.

Having put the steeping liquid and the malt extract in the pot, you now must add some water. Fill the pot to a level that will give you enough space to allow for a very fast, rolling boil. There should also be enough space at the top to give you room should a boilover occur. Slowly bring the liquids to a boil, stirring regularly to mix all of the liquids well. Once you have achieved a nice rolling boil, watch out for the boilover and reduce the heat until you reach a consistent boil that is not too rapid. You may now add your boiling/bittering hops. You must boil this mixture for a minimum of 45 minutes and no longer than 1 hour.

Be very consistent with your boiling time each time you repeat a recipe or you will see a change in the quality and the characteristics of your brew.

If a recipe calls for flavoring hops, they should be added three-quarters way through the boil. (Again be careful with your timing when repeating recipes.)

Once you have completed the boil, turn off the heat, add your finishing hops if the recipe calls for them, cover the container and allow the mixture to finish with a lid on for about 10 minutes.

Next you must prepare to pitch your yeast. If you are using a carboy as a frementation vessel, you must temper the glass or you will have some serious glass breakage. Warm the carboy by pouring warm water over the *outside* of the vessel. If you are using plastic, no need to warm it.

Add your wort to the fermentation vessel and top up the container with cold water to a level that is consistent with previous instructions in this book (page 48). Once the temperature in the vessel has dropped to 80°F, you may pitch the yeast into the fermentation vessel. Aerate the liquid to begin the activation process. If you are using a carboy, you can rock it from side to side to agitate the liquid and if using a plastic fermenter, use a sterilized/sanitized spoon to stir the liquid. After this, connect the fermentation/air lock and let the fermentation begin at room temperature.

Refer back to the section of basic home brewing beginning on page 36 for the procedures to follow from here.

# 7

# *FINE FOOD, FINE BEER*

*F*or many years now, beer has been relegated to the gastronomic back burner, used as a last resort when people talked about food and the appropriate beverage to marry it with. But now we have seen that beer is a fine accompaniment with all foods. You just have to find the right one. Over the centuries, wine has been discussed as the ideal beverage to work with food and to this day there are still experiments happening in homes throughout the world on a daily (nightly) basis. Well, now we have started to take beer as a serious food drink. It *can* work and it *does* work beautifully. Experimentation is the key and a knowledge of food and the style of beer is essential for creating a harmonious meal.

The popularity of beer and food matching is blossoming nationally and internationally with restaurants, brew pubs and breweries leading the world to an eye opening experience. Many restaurants have realized the profitability of hosting beer/food tasting events on a regular basis. It allows them to educate their current customers while it brings in new patrons who have a love of beer or who want to learn more. Wine dinners have served a similar function for restaurateurs and they don't want to see any opportunity slip by.

All of this has been a boon for those of us who love good beer and good food. We can now sit down to a wonderful dinner, learn more about beer and its production, enjoy fine food and meet new people with the same interests we have. What better way to spend an evening? Following are a few menus from some recent beer dinners. I hope they will give you some ideas for future consideration.

*THE FRIENDS LAKE INN*, Chestertown, New York

> *Appetizer:* Chicken and Green Chili Burrito
> with Roasted Corn and Tomatillo Salsa
> *Beer:* Grant's India Pale Ale
>
> *Soup:* Broth of Roasted Red Peppers with Oysters
> and Andouille Sausage
> *Beer:* Cellis White Ale
>
> *Entrée:* Char-Roasted Rack of Lamb with Chipotle
> Maple Syrup, with Cinnamon-scented Basmati Rice
> and Fried Plantain
> *Beer:* Sierra Nevada Big Foot Ale
>
> *Dessert:* Chocolate Custard with Espresso Caramel
> *Beer:* Blackwell Stout

*THE FRENCHTOWN INN,* Frenchtown, New Jersey
   *Featuring:* Young's Brewery from Great Britain

   *Hors d'oeuvre:* Special London Ale

   *First Course:* Beer Battered Gulf Shrimp with
      Country Cole Slaw, Remoulade Sauce and
      Fingerling Potatoes
   *Beer:* Ram Rod Pale Ale

   *Entrée:* Brisket of Beef with Horseradish Coulis
      topped with Melted English Cheddar Cheese
   *Beer:* Oatmeal Stout

   *Dessert:* Stilton Cheese, Sliced Apples, Walnut Diamonds
      drizzled with Caramel Sauce
   *Beer:* "Old Nick" Barley Wine


*THE RITZ CARLTON HOTEL,* Philadelphia, Pennsylvania

   *First Course:* Rabbit Terrine with Celery Root,
      Asparagus, Portobello Mushrooms and Branch
      Creek Greens
   *Beer:* Pilsener Urquell

   *Soup:* Oyster-Stout Bisque with Samuel Smith's
      Oatmeal Stout
   *Beer:* Anchor Porter

*Sorbet:* Pear and Frozen Raspberries
*Beer:* Lindeman's Framboise Lambic

*Entrée:* Braised Lamb Shank with Barley and
　　Caramelized Spring Onions
*Beer:* Dock Street Maibock

*Dessert:* Chocolate-Orange Decadence,
　　Hazelnut Biscotti
*Beer:* Mackeson Triple Stout

*Digestif:* Brasserie Dubuisson "Scaldis"


*THE FRENCHTOWN INN*, Frenchtown, New Jersey

Assorted Hors d'oeuvre
*Beer:* Samuel Smith's Winter Welcome

*Soup:* Smoked Cheddar Cheese Soup with a
　　Grilled Chicken Quesadilla
*Beer:* Rogue "Mogul" Ale

*Entrée:* A Traditional Shepherds Pie
*Beer:* Samuel Smith's Imperial Stout

*Dessert:* Pumpkin Tart with a Shortbread Crust
　　with a Candied Ginger Chantilly Cream
*Beer:* Hürlimann "Samichlaus" Dark Lager

What we are beginning to see, finally, is a groundswell of enthusiasm by lovers of fine brews and food. This probably has roots in the baby boom generation, as it did for wine and food, due to the lack of interesting beer available commercially. This group of people was frustrated by bland and innocuous brews and began to search the world as they traveled or read. They found that there were interesting beers and that a cuisine seemed to evolve around those particular styles of beer.

If we take a look at specific areas of beer production (which we will), we can see that the beer and food began to find each other and that there is a harmonious marriage happening. In America, we are experiencing a huge culinary awakening, finding much pleasure in discovering the roots of our culinary heritage. The beauty is that we have so many diverse cultures coming together in our nation – so the possibilities are endless.

As the menus above illustrate, there is a multicultural dining experience reigning in America. Accordingly, there are many different styles of beer available. Home brewed, microbrewed or commercially brewed – it is becoming easier to find the right brew to work with fine foods.

There are many areas in Europe that have cuisines which work perfectly with the locally brewed beer. Was this a natural occurrence or was it that the chefs, through experimentation, came up with the perfect dish to match the local brew? One imagines it was a little of both – due to climate, soils, access to the sea and nearby animals and grains, local beer would share traits with local cuisine and that incongruities would be smoothed over by the skillful chef and brewer working together.

Commencing your education along the beer and food road in your home kitchen is probably the best way to learn. From there, as you become familiar with the food ingredients and the styles of beer, you can begin to experiment and develop your own recipes and pairings.

From England and her brewers and chefs, we have gained the knowledge that oysters and other shellfish with their briny, salty and tangy qualities work nicely with a rich, creamy, yet dry stout or porter. Why does this work and how does this marriage compare to the classic food and wine marriage of Muscadet (Loire Valley) or Chablis (Burgundy) and shellfish?

With the wines, it is the balance of fruit and acidity that seems to balance and marry with the shellfish. The acid and the brininess do not clash, as one might think. The dry stout and porter seem to enhance the saltiness and briny attributes of the seafood and the richness adds a special balance on the palate. If you live on the East Coast of the United States and have access to hard shell blue crab from the Chesapeake Bay, try steamed crabs in the middle of the summer along with an assortment of stouts or – for a new experience – a crisp German-style wheat beer, with its citrusy, clovelike aromas.

## STEAMED HARD SHELL CRABS, TIDEWATER STYLE
Recipe for 12 hearty appetites

> *5 dozen hard shell blue crabs, alive and kicking*
> *1 small can Old Bay Seasoning (you may need more if*
> *     you want the spiciness to be more pronounced)*
> *black pepper, freshly ground, to taste*
> *kosher salt, to taste*
> *1 tablespoon red pepper flakes (optional)*
> *1 tablespoon mustard seed, crushed*
> *1 tablespoon celery seed, crushed*
> *2 12-ounce bottles stout*
> *1 quart water or fish stock*
> *1 large pot with a lid for steaming crabs*
> *colander or steaming rack*
> *lots of newspaper and a picnic table*

Mix all of the dry ingredients well in a large stainless steel bowl. Place the liquid ingredients in the large pot and bring to a boil. Place the steaming rack or colander in the bottom of the pot. The next part can be a little tricky a – the blue crabs have strong, nasty, little pincher claws, so beware. If possible, rub the crabs on the top and bottoms of their bodies with the dried mixture and place them in three or four layers in the pot. Alternatively, you can place one layer and rub the tops with the dry mixture, followed by each successive layer. Steam the crabs in batches until they are bright orange/red. They are cooked at this point. As they are finished, place them in a large bowl and put them out for your guests. The crabs will need a few minutes to cool and in that time you can be starting the following batches.

Cover the table with newspaper, supply wooden hammers for cracking the claws and shells and small cocktail forks for extracting the meat. After all of the crabs have finished cooking, you might want to bring the liquid in the pot to the table for dipping. It will have reduced nicely and absorbed some of the seasonings that fell through. This is a great way to enjoy a summer afternoon or evening and experience a special food and beer interplay.

When eating the spicy and sometimes fiery hot cuisines of the Far East, most people who drink wine will ask for a beer. The reason is that they refuse to try some very winning combinations like Sauvignon Blanc, Riesling or a light, fruity, low-tannin red wine like a Beaujolais. The Thais are the masters of delicately seasoned foods that also pack a good deal of heat. They also have a very fine beer in a lager style called Singha that marries quite well with many native dishes. For an interesting evening of food and beer try the following recipe:

### GAI YAHNG (Grilled chicken)

This is a very simple dish, though you will need to prepare two of the condiments in advance.

> ½ cup cilantro paste (recipe and ingredients follow)
> 3 tablespoons light soy sauce (available in Chinese markets)
> salt and pepper to taste
> 1 chicken, cut up into sections, or breasts, thighs or, even better,
>     wings (for an Asian version of Buffalo wings)
> Hot and Sweet Garlic Sauce, for dipping (recipe and ingredients follow)

For the cilantro paste: 2 bunches fresh cilantro (Chinese parsley), washed and chopped with a portion of the stems; 2 teaspoons of whole white peppercorns, ground; ½ cup of roasted peanuts, finely chopped; 4 cloves of garlic, peeled and finely chopped; 2 tablespoons of dark sesame oil; ¼ cup of Singha or similar-style beer. Combine all ingredients in a blender or food processor and blend quickly by pulsing a few times. This mixture may be refrigerated for up to one week. Yields about 1 cup.

    For the Hot and Sweet Garlic Sauce: ½ cup water; 1 cup sugar; ¼ cup rice vinegar; ¼ cup white vinegar; 3 cloves garlic, peeled and finely chopped; dash of salt and black pepper; 1 tablespoon of dried red chilis, coarsely ground or finely chopped (available at oriental food markets). Place the water, sugar, rice and white vinegars in a small heavy saucepan over high heat, bring to a boil and reduce the heat; stir the mixture to aid in dissolving the sugar, allow the mixture to reduce until a light syrupy texture is achieved. Remove from the heat, stir in the chilis and taste;

adjust the seasonings if necessary with the salt and pepper. Refrigerate in a tightly sealed container. This sauce will keep for up to two weeks. Yields about 1½ cups.

Now for the chicken:

Place your cut up chicken parts in a bowl or container with a lid just large enough to accommodate all the pieces. Ladle the cilantro paste, add salt and pepper, pour the soy sauce over the chicken and mix well, covering the chicken with the cilantro mixture. Cover the bowl or container and let the chicken marinate for 1 hour, remove the cover and stir the chicken around to continue the coating process. Marinate for 1 more hour. Heat up a charcoal grill or gas grill. Once the grill is hot, place chicken on grill and cook evenly for up to 45 minutes depending on the cut of chicken you are using. Remove to plates and serve with the garlic sauce. This spicy and sweet dish with herbal qualities works beautifully with the delicate, hoppy character of the Singha. Serves four and the recipes can be easily doubled.

Now that we've really got your palate and taste buds excited, let's try something a little more classic and something that goes well with a love of beef. This next dish evolved in Belgium and is a traditional dish that uses beer in the cooking process.

It is recommended that you ask your butcher for good stewing meat with very little fat and that you try to make your own veal or dark chicken stock. The canned varieties are good, but they contain salt and seem to lack the flavor of something you do at home. Kind of like home brew!

Try this dish with a Bière de Garde or a brown/dark ale-style brew.

# CARBONADE DE BOEUF À LA FLAMANDE

(Beef stew in a Flemish style)

*2½ lbs beef for stewing, cut into bite-size pieces*
*2 tablespoons flour*
*6 shallots or 3 small onions, roughly chopped*
*½ stick butter or about 3 ounces of olive oil*
*1 garlic clove, finely chopped*
*1 tablespoon fresh chopped tarragon*
*2 tablespoons fresh chopped thyme*
*1 tablespoon imported Dijon or whole-grain mustard*
*Salt and pepper*
*3 cups of brown or dark ale*
*2 cups veal or dark chicken stock*
*1 heavy casserole with a lid*

Heat the casserole over high heat, place your beef in a bowl and toss with the flour to coat lightly. Place the butter or oil in the casserole, just enough to coat the pan's bottom; add the beef in small batches and brown on all sides, remove to a bowl until all the beef has been browned; add the remaining butter or oil and sauté the shallots or onions and cook for a few minutes; add the herbs and the garlic, cook for 2 minutes, stirring frequently. Deglaze the pan with the beer and scrape the pan to remove all of those wonderful particles. Add 1 cup of the veal stock and place the beef back into the casserole. Bring to a boil and reduce the heat until you have a slight simmer. Place the lid on the casserole and cook the meat at simmer for about 1 hour. Remove the beef and transfer it to a container with a lid on top. Heat the sauce to a boil and reduce until it has a nice glossy consistency. If you feel the sauce needs more stock for flavoring, use the remaining 1 cup of veal stock and reduce. To finish, add the mustard and stir it in well; adjust the seasoning with the salt and pepper. Serve with egg noodles or boiled potatoes tossed with some butter and parsley and some pan-braised Belgian endive.

This makes a super dinner on a cool fall evening or a cold winter's night, sitting by a fire with some friends or loved ones. Serves four people and can be doubled quite easily. Remember to reduce the liquid to a nice glossy consistency.

The Belgians love their mussels and no trip through the world of food and beer would be complete without another simple and flavorful marriage of beer and fruits of the sea. In Belgium, every corner and street has a restaurant, café, brasserie or bar with some version of mussels on its menu. The proximity to the North Sea is why the Belgians adore their seafood in all of its guises.

Beer selection will differ depending on the type of fish and the individual preparation. This mussel dish is traditionally served with Gueuze, which is a blending of young and old lambics that has a wonderful Champagne-like character. Alternatively, you can use a farmhouse-style or Trappist-style brew. The French, by the way, would be horrified at serving beer with a dish that they normally associate with a light and refreshing white wine. There are plenty of other types of beers that would also go swimmingly with this delicate preparation of Belgium's favorite mollusk.

# MOULES À LA BIÈRE (Mussels cooked in beer)

*estimate about 10 mussels per person for a first course*
*or 18 mussels per person for an entrée-size serving*
*8 shallots, finely chopped*
*2 cloves garlic, finely chopped*
*2 ounces butter or 3 ounces of extra virgin olive oil*
*½ cup washed and chopped flat leaf parsley*
*1½ cup Gueuze or other fine lambic or ale*
*lots of good crunchy French-style or farm bread for sopping up the liquid*
*1 pot with a lid large enough to accommodate the mussels*

Wash mussels well in cold water and scrub to remove the "beard" from the mussel; discard any with cracked shells. Most mussels you buy today have been farm raised by new aqua-culture methods and they are much cleaner than mussels were ten years ago. Heat the pot over high heat, add the butter or oil, add the shallots and sauté until translucent. Add the garlic and cook for only a minute, add the beer and parsley and heat to a boil. At last, add the mussels and cover with a lid.

Cook the mussels, stirring regularly for about 8 to 10 minutes or until the shells are opened. Transfer the mussels to good sized soup bowls and ladle the cooking liquid over them. Be sure to discard any mussels that have not opened. Serve with the bread. In Belgium, the other national dish that is normally served with this recipe is very thinly sliced potatoes cooked like French fries. Get ready for a fun-filled evening. This is a great dish to serve in the late spring or early fall because that is when the mussels are at their plumpest and best.

In the Alsace area of France, which borders Germany along the Rhine river, are some of the best vineyards, the best restaurants and some wonderful beers to marry with the distinct indigenous cuisine. The brews from this area vary in style from light ale up to rich and creamy potations that go wonderfully with dessert. I have had a couple of very nice pilsener types that worked beautifully with the hearty and flavorful dish below:

## CHOUCROUTE À L'ALSACIENNE
(Sauerkraut with pork and sausage)

> *3 lbs sauerkraut*
> *½ lb excellent quality smoked bacon, sliced ½-inch thick and cut into cubes*
> *1 teaspoon caraway seeds*
> *1 onion, finely chopped*
> *1 carrot, peeled and finely chopped*
> *1 clove garlic, peeled and finely chopped*
> *2 tablespoons flat-leaf parsley, washed and chopped fine*
> *2 tablespoons fresh thyme, finely chopped*
> *1 bay leaf*
> *pepper to taste*
> *4 smoked pork chops, cut ¾-inch thick*
> *4 garlic and pork – or preferably duck or other game – sausages*
> *1 cup of veal or dark chicken stock – this will be used only if*
>     *after cooking you feel you need the dish a bit moister*
> *1 12-ounce bottle hoppy pilsener-style beer*
>     *(Philadelphia's Dock Street would work well)*
> *1 large, ovenproof casserole with a lid, large enough to*
>     *accommodate all the ingredients*

To begin, heat the casserole on high heat, add the bacon and reduce the heat to medium. Cook the bacon until it is almost crisp; add the onion and carrots and sauté until the onion is translucent. Add the garlic, caraway, parsley, thyme and bay leaf and sauté for about 2 minutes to incorporate well. Add the sauerkraut and cook for a few minutes, stirring to mix all the ingredients. Transfer to a container.

Preheat your oven at 350°F. Turn the heat on the burner back to high and sear the pork chops briefly on both sides until just brown. Remove to a plate. Add the sausages and sear on all sides over medium heat. Remove and deglaze the pan by adding the beer. Scrape up all the particles. Add the sauerkraut in a thin layer, top with two chops and two sausages, add another layer of sauerkraut and another layer of meats, finish with any of the remaining sauerkraut. Place the lid on top and place the casserole in the preheated oven and cook for about 1 to 1½ hours.

During the cooking process, check the casserole and see if it needs any liquid. It shouldn't, but if it does, add a bit of the stock. Serve this warming and comforting dish with freshly mashed potatoes or parsleyed new potatoes. Serves four and can be doubled.

In the region of France just south of the famed Côte d'Or in Burgundy lies the Beaujolais district. This wine region is renowned for its wonderfully fruity red wines made from the Gamay grape and also for a very regional dish, *Coq au Vin*. This recipe was no doubt created by the farm cook trying to find a way to use that old rooster running around the farmyard. The wine helps to break down the toughness of the old bird. In the north of France, where wine grapes won't grow, the chefs and cooks had to adapt their recipes using beer and it certainly does work well with a Bière de Garde or a Trappist-style ale from the Flemish area just across the border. Today, most of the chickens we eat are very young and tender so there is no need for a long stewing to tenderize the bird. A moderate length of time is all that is necessary.

# POULET À LA BIÈRE DU NORD
(Chicken stewed with beer from the north)

*1 4-lb chicken, cut up into sections*
*olive oil*
*12 pearl onions, peeled*
*2 carrots, peeled and cut into ½-inch pieces*
*12 large mushrooms, cleaned and cut into quarters*
*1 clove garlic, peeled and finely chopped*
*2 tablespoons of fresh tarragon, finely chopped*
*2 cups dark chicken stock*
*pepper and salt to taste*
*12 ounces Bière de Garde-style ale or ale of similar quality*
*1 cup heavy cream (optional)*
*1 oven-proof casserole with a lid, large enough to*
*accommodate the ingredients*

Preheat oven to 350°F. Place casserole on a burner, add olive oil to coat the bottom and heat over medium high heat. Very lightly pepper and salt the chicken pieces on both sides. Place two or three pieces of the chicken in the heated casserole; brown both sides and transfer to a plate. Complete the process with all of the chicken pieces and reserve until later.

Add the onions, carrots and mushrooms and cook for about 6 minutes stirring regularly; add the garlic and the tarragon and cook for a minute, stirring to incorporate the ingredients. Add the beer and scrape up the good particles on the bottom of the casserole. Reduce the liquid for a few minutes at a slow boil, add the chicken stock and bring to a boil over high heat. Once this has boiled, add the chicken pieces and place the casserole, with a cover, into the preheated oven and cook for 1 hour or until the chicken is done.

Remove the chicken from the casserole and place on a serving platter and cover to keep warm. Put the casserole back on the burner, on high heat, taste to see if it needs more salt and pepper, adjust seasoning and reduce the liquid until you have a nice, glossy texture. If you are using the heavy cream, you should add it now and reduce the liquid again. Pour the sauce over the chicken and vegetables. Serve this with the beer and braised salsify, a white carrotlike tuber that is wonderful with this dish. You could also serve a potato gratin as well. Serves four and can be doubled.

Japan is a huge consumer of beer of all styles and some of its largest breweries make very fine quality beers that express the flavors of the styles beautifully. Some of the largest brewers are even experimenting at company operated micro-breweries to develop old world styles of beer for limited production runs.

Japan is also one of the largest consumers of fresh seafood, raw and cooked. The dish below, in its traditional form, calls for a reasonably heavy salting technique called *furi-jo*. We have adapted it to take into account our new health consciousness and also the freshness of fish available to us. This dish would be ideally suited to a wheat or pilsener beer, but please don't let that deter you from experimenting. How about a stout, given the salty qualities of this dish?

### *SUZUKI SHIO-YAKI* (Salt-grilled sea bass)

*2 lbs sea bass or red snapper filets*
*2 red bell peppers, quartered and seeded*
*kosher salt, freshly ground*
*bamboo or wood skewers about 12 inches long*
*vegetable oil for the peppers and the grill*
*4 lemon wedges, for garnish*
*pickled ginger or pickled ginger shoots, for garnish*

Buy the freshest fish possible from a reputable fishmonger. If possible, avoid supermarkets – they never seem to have anyone who has the innate abilities or fondness that a small owner-operated store has. When you get the fish home and are ready to prepare it, remove any bones that may have been missed by the purveyor, using tweezers or needle-nose pliers.

Pat the filets dry with a towel and then proceed to cut them into pieces about 4 inches in length. Lightly salt the pieces on both sides. You can salt the skin side a bit heavier. Place them on a plate and let stand for a half hour in the refrigerator.

Heat your charcoal or gas grill until very hot. Place the quartered peppers on skewers and rub with oil. Next, thread the skewers, two per piece, evenly spaced, through the fish filets, one filet per set of skewers. Oil the grill surface to avoid sticking. For insurance, you might want to oil the fish ever so lightly. Next, grill the fish, skin side down, for about 5 minutes. Gently remove the filets from the grill and re-oil it before placing the filets skin side up. Place filets, skin side up, on grill and cook for another 2 to 3 minutes.

While you are grilling the fish, you can also be grilling the peppers. They will take about 5 minutes and should be just getting slightly brown when cooked. Remove the fish and peppers and place them on individual plates, one filet and two pepper quarters per person. Garnish the plates with the lemon and the ginger and serve with red rice. Red rice is a mixture of azuki beans, rice and black sesame seeds. Serves four and can be doubled easily.

And now it's time for some cross-cultural cooking. My wife and I have an absolute love of the foods and herbs from the south of France. Additionally, my wife's family traces its heritage back to Osceola, of the Seminole nation, in Charleston, South Carolina. We have had a number of wonderful dinners in both regions and have created some interesting and simple dishes using ingredients and recipes indigenous to both areas. The most recent was a dinner combining grouper, *herbes de Provence* and a traditional New Year's dish, Hoppin' John. We had the meal with Mark Rosner's home-brewed wheat beer recipe from Brunswick Brewing Supply.

# GROUPER FILET WITH HERBES DE PROVENCE

*4 grouper or swordfish filets, about 8 ounces per filet*
*8 shallots, peeled and thinly sliced*
*3 cloves garlic, peeled and finely chopped*
*1 cup Niçoise-style olives, unpitted*
*3 plum tomatoes, sliced in half, seeds removed and chopped fine*
*3 tablespoons herbes de Provence (sold in fine food stores)*
*4 tablespoons extra virgin olive oil*
*12 ounces wheat or other light-style beer*
*1 cup fish or shrimp stock, or light chicken stock*
*salt and pepper to taste*
*1 recipe Hoppin' John*

Remove any bones from the grouper filets that your fish store may have missed using tweezers or needle-nose pliers. Pat the fish dry using a towel. Season all sides with 2 tablespoons of the herbes de Provence and a little of the pepper.

Heat a large nonstick sauté pan over high heat. When the pan is quite hot, add 1 to 2 tablespoons oil to coat the pan lightly. Turn the heat down to medium high and put the filets skin side up into the pan. Sauté until they are nicely browned and will remove easily from the pan – about 5 to 8 minutes. If you are using swordfish, it will take less time to cook. Turn the filets and continue cooking for about 4 to 5 minutes. Transfer to an ovenproof pan and place in a warm oven, 200°F to 225°F, to hold for the completion of the sauce.

Turn the heat up to high on the burner and add the remaining oil. Add the onion, cook for 4 minutes and stir to scrape up any particles of fish. Add the garlic, herbes de Provence, olives and tomatoes and cook for 3 minutes to incorporate all of the ingredients. Add the beer and reduce this for a few minutes. Add the stock and bring to a boil.

Reduce the heat to medium and reduce the volume of liquid by half. Place the fish filets on warmed dinner plates and spoon the sauce on the sides surrounding the fish. Do not pour sauce over the top of the fish— you want to preserve that crisp top layer.

Serve with Hoppin' John, a classic New Year's dish south of the Mason-Dixon line, but especially in South Carolina. A recipe can be found in any good cook book that covers the cuisines of the South. Serves four and can be doubled easily.

One of my favorite styles of beer is a dark lager and one of the better ones is from Brazil. Xingu has a beautiful, dark amber color from the heavily roasted malts and an almost licorice coffee taste. It goes wonderfully with the highly seasoned foods of South and Central America. One recipe that I have always enjoyed playing around with is black bean soup.

### *SOPA DE FREJOLES NEGROS* (Black bean soup)

*2 lbs dried black beans, soaked in cold water to cover for 1 hour*
*3 tablespoons olive oil*
*1 large onion, peeled and finely chopped*
*3 cloves garlic, peeled and finely chopped*
*2 carrots, peeled and finely chopped*
*2 celery stalks, washed and finely chopped*
*1 teaspoon ground cumin*
*1 teaspoon ground coriander seed*
*1 teaspoon ground cardamom*
*1 bay leaf*
*1 whole smoked ham hock, not cut up*
*Tabasco sauce to taste*
*2 quarts chicken or vegetable stock*
*12 ounces dark lager or similar style beer*
*salt and pepper to taste*
*8 teaspoons sour cream, for garnish*
*8 sprigs fresh cilantro, for garnish*
*1 heavy-gauge soup pot with a lid*
*blender or food processor (optional)*

Place the soup pot on a burner set to high. Once hot, add oil and sauté the onions over medium high heat until they begin to brown lightly. Add the carrots, garlic and celery and cook while stirring for 2 minutes. Add the cumin, coriander, cardamom, bay leaf and ham hock, stir for two minutes until the spices have been well incorporated and have released some of their flavorings. Add a few shakes of the red pepper sauce to taste now or you can wait until it has finished cooking. If added now, it will season the soup nicely.

Pour in the beer and reduce the liquid for 2 minutes. Add the beans and their soaking water and 1 quart of the stock, reserving the remainder for later. Cover and bring to a boil. Once boiling, reduce the heat until you achieve a slow boil.

Cover the pot only by about 75 percent so that the soup may reduce. Stir the soup every 15 minutes and check for volume reduction. Remove the ham hock after the soup has cooked for about 30 minutes. Add the remaining quart of stock and continue cooking at a slow boil.

Cook the soup for about 1 hour. Remove the meat from the ham hock, cut it up into a small dice and return it to the soup. Finish cooking the soup for about another 15 minutes. Check the seasoning and add salt and pepper and the Tabasco, if you like.

At this point, you can serve the soup as is or you can take about ⅔ of the vegetables and beans and purée them in the blender or food processor. Once this is completed, ladle the soup into bowls and garnish with a teaspoon of the sour cream and a sprig of the cilantro. Serves eight for a soup course or four for a dinner-size portion. The soup may be prepared up to three days in advance and refrigerated. It will definitely improve with a few days of age to allow a full melding of flavors. For a true South American evening, follow the soup with the Argentinean beef dish Metambre los Pampas (No Hunger on the Prairie). This is made by rolling thinly sliced flank steak around hard boiled eggs, gherkins and onions and slow roasting in the oven.

To conclude this section, it is necessary to reiterate that you should at all times keep an open mind to the beer and food possibilities every time you open a bottle or cook a meal. There are no hard rules, there are only the questions: Do you like it and does it taste good?

Without experimentation, where would the home brewer and chef be? Keep an open mind and try to think logically about the style of beer you wish to drink. Consider your ingredients and what affect they might have on the brew. It's only a great home brew with a great meal. It'll work one way or another. Enjoy!

# 8

# *TASTING YOUR BREW*

*T*he serving of your brew will be very important to you and the people you share your beer with. Two points deserve your close attention when serving home brew: sediment and temperature.

Sediment is an inevitable part of homemade beer. As we've said, it won't *hurt* you to consume sediment, but too much of it can sour the flavor of your beer and a whole lot of it can make you sick to your stomach. The trick, then, is to get the beer out of the bottle and leave the sediment.

To accomplish the pouring, handle the bottle carefully once you are ready to open it. Try to use a glass that will accommodate a whole bottle's worth of brew so that you don't stir up the sediment on the second or third pour. If you must pour into two or more glasses, keep the bottle in the same horizontal position when traveling from glass to glass which guarantee a clean fill. Take your time and pick the right glass. A tall and slender glass will help head retention better than a short, squat one. Appearance really does enhance the tasting experience.

Most Americans are used to drinking their beer (and wine, by the way) cold – too cold in fact. Chilliness does nothing to promote the quality of the beverage. We are a nation of soda pop drinkers accustomed to ice cold drinks. We must educate ourselves about the pleasures that can be derived from drinking beer and wine at the *optimal* temperature.

Most refrigerators, whether they be a commercial or home variety, are set to about 39°F to 42°F so that food will not spoil. This is too cold for almost all of the beers produced at home or commercially. The ideal is a refrigerator used only for the storage of beer and wine, set at the higher temperatures the beverages require. Since this is almost impossible for most people's budgets and space, there are alternatives. When you feel like having a beer, take it out of the refrigerator and let it stand at room temperature for 10 minutes or so to allow it to come up a few degrees. The alternative is to take a warm beer from its storage area and place it in the fridge for about half an hour or so to allow it to go down in temperature to the desired level.

Over the years, through much experimentation, there has emerged an estimate of desirable temperature ranges for each type of beer. We suggest strongly that you try a brew ice cold and then try one that has been brought to the ideal temperature and experience the improvement yourself. Here are some guidelines:

Light and pale lager/pilseners 45°F to 50°F
Amber and dark lager/pilseners 55°F to 60°F
Pale ales 45°F to 55°F
Dark ales 50°F to 55°F
Porters and stouts 55°F to 60°F

When your brew is at the ideal temperature you will notice good head retention as well the ability of the carbonation to bring about that smoothness and balance of flavor that are sought in a well-made beer.

## EVALUATING BEERS

As you begin to enjoy beer more and more, you will wish to begin to evaluate each one systematically – especially your home brews. If you don't step back a bit and take a long, objective look at your creations, you won't be able to perfect your abilities to craft a great home brew.

There are many different types and styles of beer that you should become familiar with to open your mind and to educate your palate. The best way to educate yourself is by tasting beer frequently – on its own and with food. The most objective way to taste is in a very scientific and precise manner.

Have a clean and well-lit area with as few disturbances from outside influences as possible. Taste with friends and fellow brewers, but always be aware that other tasters may have slightly different impressions of the beer in question. Over the years, tasters have come up with basic rating guidelines for beer. It is important to have a good overall knowledge of the specific qualities that you will be evaluating in the beer. These include:

1) Appearance
2) Aroma and/or bouquet
3) Taste
4) Final impression

Many tasters of beer or wine automatically want to assign *numerical* ratings to the beverage. I strongly suggest that you not get into the habit of rating brews by a score of 1 to 20 or 1 to 100 or any other numerical scoring, unless you wish to begin the qualification process to become a judge of competitions. Evaluating your beer is supposed to be an enjoyable and a learning experience – not a contest. Your comments and impressions are more important than some score.

*APPEARANCE:* When looking at the brew, does it have the proper color for the style of beer you have created? Does it appear cloudy from particulate matter, such as sediment? Has it developed a chill haze from the protein remaining in the beer? Does the beer show proper head retention for the style?

*AROMA AND/OR BOUQUET:* There is call for discussion here as some people prefer to distinguish between aroma and bouquet. Some believe that the aroma comes from the malts and grains while bouquet comes from the hops. Others don't even mention bouquet and assign aroma to the overall impression of the malts, grains, hops and other adjuncts used.

I am of the latter school. I always think of, and associate, bouquet with wines that have been aged properly in a cellar and have developed "bouquet." For beer, the only exception I would make is for barley wines, Bière de Gardes, imperial stouts and others that take well to cellaring. These brews certainly develop different aromas and a distinct "bouquet" as they age.

Aromas that you will be looking for in your brew will, as always, depend on the style of beer that you are evaluating. Aromas most associated with beer are caramel, roasted and toasted qualities, maltlike sweetness, chocolate, butterscotch, apples, citrus, pears, tropical fruits, grapefruit and plenty more. If you smell aromas that are unpleasant, such as those bacteria bring, then you should certainly characterize the beer as not acceptable and it should be strictly analyzed to determine where the problems originated.

*TASTE:* Everyone has his or her own impressions about how a beer will taste, but there are certain absolute standards to be considered.

Biologically, we all have the same perceptions once the beer hits our tongue and mouth and there are definite things that we know without really *thinking* about them. The tip of the tongue lets us know if the beer is sweet or dry. The sides, toward the front of the tongue, will tell us if it is salty or not. The next perception on the sides of the tongue and the mouth is that of an acidic/astringent/sour component. And finally, at the back of the mouth and tongue is where we get bitter notes and also the final impression of the beer. As with wine, beer should be swirled about the mouth to reach all parts of the palate.

Here are some general questions you should ask yourself as you further evaluate the taste of beer:

*SWEETNESS:* Does this level of sweetness or lack thereof work for the style of beer? Is the sweet impression from the malting or the hops or is it some (possibly detrimental) byproduct of the brewing process? Is the beer *meant* to be sweet or has the fermenting gone awry?

*SALTINESS:* Are you getting a perceived saltlike taste because of the minerals that were in the water? Does this impression work with the style of beer? Or does it clash and lead to a poor final impression of the beer?

*ACIDITY/ASTRINGENCY/SOURNESS:* Does this come about because of excessive carbonation? Is it pleasant with the style of beer? Is it due to a bacterial contaminant, such as acetic acid, which is the acid found in vinegars?

*BITTERNESS:* Is the beer too bitter because it was overhopped? Is it astringent due to the tannins that can come from the grains and their husks? Does the bitterness work with the other flavor components?

*FINAL IMPRESSION:* This is where the rubber meets the road. Do you like the beer after all of the analysis? Does everything work together? Is there one component that is too pronounced? Does the beer create a nice long finish after it has been swallowed? Would you want a second glass and would you want to consume it with food?

It might be worthwhile to create a chart to help you to evaluate your beers as you begin to craft them (and learn to sample other beers knowledgeably). This chart could be kept with your journal notes for each beer so that you have a continuing record of each beer you make. A short and simple form with an area to make notes and comments about every aspect of your brew is important. Below is an example of one that might help you.

# HOME BREW EVALUATION FORM

Beer:                           Style:

Production Dates:               Date of Evaluation:

Appearance:

    Color

    Clarity

    Head Retention/Formation

    General Impressions for the Style

Aroma Profile:

    Malt Aromas

    Hop Aromas

    Adjunct Aromas

    Defective Odors/Aromas

    General Impressions for the Style

Flavor Profile:

    Sweetness

    Saltiness/Mineral

    Acidity/Sour/Astringent

    Bitterness

    Malt Impact

    Body (light/medium/full)

    Carbonation

    Flavor Impression

    Flavor Problems

    General Impressions of the Style

Final Impression:

    Finish (short/medium/long)

    Flavors on Finish

    Problems Related to Finish

    Typical of the Style

    Would you drink another glass/bottle?

    What would you like to eat with this beer?

    Would you brew another beer from the same recipe?

    Final Flavor Impressions

# 9

# COLLECTING BREWERIANA

*T*he hobby of collecting brewery memorabilia has been growing dramatically for the past twenty years and collectors can be found all over the world. In the most recent membership directory of the National Association of Breweriana Advertising (N.A.B.A.), members are listed from every state of the United States, Guam, England, Canada, Belgium, Holland and Sweden.

All countries that produce beer have avid collectors searching for some sort of memorabilia. The memorabilia collected includes labels from bottles and kegs, mugs, glasses, beer trays, bottle openers of all types, model trucks, clocks, coasters, public stock certificates issued by the breweries, old photos, cans, bottles, historical records, matchboxes and holders, keg taps and pulls, anything related to pre-Prohibition brewing, and the list goes on and on. It seems that anything and everything associated with the history and lore of beer can become a collectible item.

N.A.B.A. members meet once a year for an annual convention and it is always in or near a city with a rich history of brewing. At a typical convention held near Pittsburgh, attendees had the opportunity to tour breweries, trade or buy memorabilia and generally socialize with people of the same ilk. Many are amateur brewers as well, and have developed vast collections through their love of beer and brewing.

Frank J. Mrazik of Canada has a collection that includes more than 150,000 labels with examples from every beer-producing country in the world. Mr. Mrazik began collecting matchbook covers more than forty years ago and became interested in beer labels more recently. He has since developed the world's largest collection of Canadian brewery labels and is constantly on the hunt for more to add to his holdings. He recently made a trip to Vermont just to visit its micro-breweries to ensure that he had their labels in his collection.

It has become Mrazik's passion to have every label from every brewery in his collection. He admits this is almost a Herculean or maybe a Sisyphean task, but it is something that he does with honest zeal. A retired food technologist, Mrazik spends almost all of his time communicating by letter (hundreds per year) and phone with breweries and other collectors.

In the 1930s, "Uncle Ernie" Oest began collecting beer labels while working in his father's grocery business. By the time he sold his collection a few years ago, he had amassed what was considered to be the finest collection in the world. He sold his European collection to Mr. Mrazik: more than twelve cartons of labels. Mrazik has spent hundreds of hours cataloging it by year, country of origin and town.

Like other memorabilia groups, breweriana collectors flock to auctions—to socialize and to compete for top-quality pieces. A typical auction in January 1995 saw phenomenal prices for some wonderful old labels. A pre-Prohibition label from Honolulu, Hawaii, went for $113 and a pre-Prohibition label from an Anheuser beer pint-size bottle sold for the remarkable price of $185. Most of the labels in this auction were in the $15 to $50 range and came from all over the United States.

There is a worldwide network of label collectors communicating regularly about new and old labels that have been added to their collections. Some of the labels are beautifully crafted and the graphics are a joy to look at. There are many clubs and societies throughout the world that catalog and help collectors to locate labels to fill out their collections. A few of them include the Labologists Club of England, the Beer Label Collectors Society of Australia and the Labolog Club of the Czech Republic.

The American Breweriana Association is another organization that offers a wide variety of information to its members and prints a bimonthly journal with loads of interesting articles.

Most of the people involved with collecting memorabilia have a love of history and study how and why breweries got started and the shifts, changes and transitions of their existence.

Of course, many of the breweries that existed during the history of the United States are no longer with us – they could not survive the Prohibition years or the competition. The history of brewing in America starts almost immediately after the first settlers arrived and there have been many books written on the subject. The first settlers came to this country with a long history and knowledge of brewing. The constant search for memorabilia concerning this history is singularly intriguing and unearthing these treasures gives great delight to those involved in this aspect of home brewing.

Another gentleman I met recently has a very large and remarkable collection of pre-Prohibition brewery advertising. His passion for collecting was sparked by a gift his wife gave him in 1973 – a book called *The Beer Book* by Will Anderson. From this chance encounter has evolved a collection of some of the most striking lithographs devoted to brewery advertising as well as glassware from German breweries, beer trays and more. Having worked for Johnson & Johnson for thirty-five years, he realized the importance of quality and craftsmanship. He has now restricted his collectibles to the pre-Prohibition period and relies on a well-developed network of friends to aid him in finding only the most revered pieces available. His other new hobby is to tour the new micro-breweries throughout in the America and also to visit some of the classic European breweries like Pilsener Urquell in the Czech Republic.

The best places to find brewing memorabilia is at local antique shows and flea markets and, naturally, at events specializing in brewery advertising. You may want to target areas that have a long brewing history because there seems to be an especially strong interest in preserving objects in the areas where breweries once prospered (and perhaps still do).

Many collectors will also go on a road trip to a new micro-brewery or a new brew pub to ensure that they have any materials that may be available to add to their collections. If these new businesses have a mailing list, make sure you are on it so that you find out about any new issues. As this era in the brewing revolution continues to evolve and grow, we can expect new and innovative advertising tools to come forth that will certainly be worth adding to a collection.

The micro-brewery industry has attracted a younger crowd of collectors who are interested in "go withs": items such as baseball caps, T-shirts, coasters and sweatshirts. This younger generation of collectors enjoy quality beers as well as the novelty of collecting advertising that usually has interesting graphics or slogans.

To get started in the breweriana (old and new) hobby, you may wish to contact the following organizations and societies:

The National Association of Breweriana Advertising
2343 Met-To-Wee Lane
Wauwatosa, Wisconsin 53226

Beer Can Collectors of America
747 Merus Court
Fenton, Missouri 63026-2092

Antique Bottle and Glass Collector
P.O. Box 187
East Greenville, Pennsylvania 18401

The American Breweriana Association
P.O. Box 11157
Pueblo, Colorado 81001

The American Museum of Brewing
The Oldenberg Brewery
I-75 at Buttermilk Place
Fort Mitchell, Kentucky 41017

Association of Brewers

P.O. Box 1679

Boulder, Colorado 80306-1679

Subsidiaries: American Homebrewers Association, Institute for Brewing Studies, Brewers Publications and Great American Beer Festival.

# SOURCES

*I*t is essential to find a knowledgeable dealer of home brewing supplies – either locally or by mail – if you are going to pursue this great pastime. The best way to locate a good one is to talk to people who brew. Also, consult the phone book or check with a good brew pub, micro-brewery or amateur brewing club. Every major city has at least one home brew supply shop and with the rising popularity of home brewing, more are opening all the time.

If you are looking for a home brew club, check with your local shop. The nationwide American Homebrewers Association in Pueblo, Colorado, lists hundreds of member organizations from around the United States. And as they say, "Relax, don't worry, have a Homebrew™."

There are so many home brew supply shops springing up that it would take douncesens of pages to list all of them. Below is a short list of some reputable suppliers that will ship almost anything you might need for home brewing. Please call them for catalogs and information.

Brunswick Brewing Supply
727 Raritan Avenue
Highland Park, New Jersey J 08904
Phone: 908-572-5353, 800-884-BREW
Large selection of brewing supplies, all-grain malts, malt extracts, hops, kits, equipment and a very knowledgeable staff to guide you along the way.

Arbor Wine and Beermaking Supplies
74 West Main Street
East Islip, New York 11730
Phone: 516-277-3004
Large selection of brewing supplies, grain malts, malt extracts, hops, equipment and kits.

The Malt Shop
North 3211 Highway South
Cascade, Wisconsin 53011
Phone: 414-528-8697, 800-235-0026
Great catalog with a vast selection of essentials and specialty items for the home brewer.

The Home Brewery™
Seven locations throughout the United States
Phone: 800-321-BREW
Offers a broad selection of items for the home brewer, thirty-two-page catalog.

# CANADA

Wine Art
Phone: 905-881-7025
Extensive supply of beer and winemaking equipment; twenty-two stores throughout Canada. Also services mail-order customers and some 400 independent stores across Canada.

The Wine Line and Beer Gear
433 Academy Road
Winnipeg, Manitoba R3N OC2
Phone: 204-489-7256

The Hopping Grape
171 Speers Road, Unit 13
Oakville, Ontario L6K 2E8
Phone: 905-845-5716

Spagnol's Wine & Beer Making Supplies
1325 Derwent Way
Annacis Island
New Westminster, British Columbia V3M 5V9
Phone: 604-524-946

# UNITED KINGDOM

The Happy Brewer
15 Union Street
MK 40255, Bedfordshire
Phone: 02-34-353-856

Cheers, Health and Homebrew
94 Priory Road
Cheam, Surrey
Phone: 081-644-0934

Harvey Wine and Beer Making
174 West Street
Faireham, Hampshire
Phone: 03-29-233-253

# BIBLIOGRAPHY

*F*ollowing is a list of publications that will be useful to the home brewer and also for those seeking general information about brewing, brew pubs, micro-breweries, clubs and more. This is only a brief list and you should check your neighborhood home brew supply shop, brew pub or micro-brewery for local publications.

*Zymurgy*
Published by the American Homebrewers Association
P.O. Box 1679
Boulder, Colorado 80306-1679
Phone: 303-447-0816
This is a very good resource for home brewers with loads of information packed into every issue. It's also well written and fun to read. You can purchase back issues relating to specific information you may need.

*Barley Corn*
P.O. Box 2328
Falls Church, Virginia 22042
Phone: 703-573-8970

*Ale Street News*
P.O. Box 1125
Maywood, New Jersey 07607
Phone: 201-368-9100

*The Malt Advocate*
3416 Oak Hill Road
Emmaus, Pennsylvania 18049
Phone: 610-967-1083

As you become more and more interested in home brewing you will undoubtedly wish to develop a library of reference books. In the books listed below you will find recipes, hints, short cuts, encouragement and lots more. Look at them as tools – inspiration when seeking out new formulas, solace when something goes badly wrong – not to mention terrific bedside reading! A few of these volumes along with a circle of home brewing associates will soon lead you to expert status.

*The Association of Brewer's Dictionary of Beer and Brewing*
Compiled by Carl Forget
Brewers Publications, 1988

*Beer: A Connoisseur's Guide to the World's Best*
Christopher Finch
Abbeville Press Publishers, 1989

*Brewing Beers Like Those You Buy*
Dave Line
G.W. Kent, Inc., 1992

*Brewing Quality Beers*
Byron Burch
Joby Press, 1986

*Brewing the World's Great Beers*
Dave Miller
Storey Communications, Inc., 1992

*The Complete Book of Home Brewing*
Dave Miller
Storey Communications, Inc., 1988

*The Essentials of Beer Styles*
Fred Eckhardt
Fred Eckhardt Communications, 1988

*The Great American Beer Cookbook*
Candy Schmerhorn
Brewers Publications, 1993

*Michael Jackson's Beer Companion*
    (plus, any other books by Michael Jackson)
Michael Jackson
Running Press, 1993

*The New Complete Joy of Home Brewing*
Charlie Papazian
Avon Books, 1984, 1991

*Principles of Brewing Science*
George Fix
Brewers Publications, 1989

*Real Beer and Good Eats: The Rebirth of America's Beer
and Food Traditions*
Bruce Aidells and Denis Kelly
Alfred A. Knopf, 1993

*Using Hops: Complete Guide to Using Hops for the Craft Brewer*
Mark Garetz
HopTech, 1994

Brewers Publications publishes a series of very sophisti-
cated books on beer styles for the home brewer. The list now
includes nine titles; at least six more are in the works. Here
is the current line-up:

*Belgian Ale* by Pierre Rajotte
*Bock* by Darryl Richman
*Continental Pilsener* by David Miller
*German Wheat Beer* by Eric Warner
*Lambic* by Jean-Xavier Guinard
*Pale Ale* by Terry Foster
*Porter* by Terry Foster
*Scotch Ale* by Greg Noonan
*Vienna, Marzen and Oktoberfest* by George and Laurie Fox

# BREWER'S LEXICON

*ADJUNCTS*: Ingredients other than sugar used for fermentation. These include rice, corn, wheat and oats. Adjuncts are often used in tandem with sugar.

*ALE*: A family of beers brewed with top-fermenting yeasts. Countless variations exist, but ale typically features more bitterness, greater strength and warmer fermentation than lager beer.

*BOCK*: German and American in origin, bock (German for goat) is a strong, dark lager traditionally served in the spring. Subspecies abound including *dopplebock* (double bock), *maibock* (May bock) and the famed *Oktoberfestbock*.

*BOTTLE CONDITIONING*: Certain beers will improve with – and may even require –additional time in the bottle undisturbed before tasting. This bottle conditining may represent the final step to a properly executed recipe.

*BREW POT:* The culinary cauldron in which a brewer makes beer. A brew pot should have at least a 5-gallon capacity and should be of the best quality available. Cheap, thin metal pots may cause the wort to burn.

*CARBOY:* Cylindrical glass fermentation container; 5- to 7-gallon capacity. Used in conjunction with a rubber stopper and fermentation lock.

*FERMENTATION:* The conversion of sugar into alcohol through the use of yeast. The crucial process in beer making.

*FERMENTATION LOCK:* Device used on a fermentation vessel. Allows gases to escape while keeping air out of the fermenter.

*HOPS:* Green, vined plants cultivated for use in beer. A traditional crop in central Europe, England and North America; may also be home-grown. Adding bitterness and aroma, hops appear in most beer recipes and are the "secret" of many legendary brews.

*HOPS, BOILING:* Hops added while the wort boils to sit for between 15 to 90 minutes, depending on the recipe. Hops are used to stabilize taste and add bitterness.

*HOPS, FINISHING:* Hops added at the very end of the wort's boil, usually to sit for one or two minutes. Provides aroma, bouquet and a distinctive, herbaceous, "hoppy" taste.

*HYDROMETER*: Indispensible brewer's tool. Measures specific gravity to determine fermentation and alcohol levels of beer as it brews.

*INTERNATIONAL BITTERNESS UNITS (I.B.U.)*: A means of rating and comparing the taste of beers. A specific I.B.U. may be listed in a recipe so that a brewer can come as close to the desired taste as possible.

*LAGER (n)*: All-encompassing term for bottom-fermented beer including pilsner, bock, and "American light" varieties. Overall, lager is lighter in strength and flavor and more carbonated than ale.

*LAGER (v)*: The process of fermenting and maturing new beer at low temperatures. Enhances smoothness and drinkability.

*MALT*: Created from partially germinated barley which is then dried and processed. Sold to home brewers in whole form or as malt extract in powdered or liquid (syrup) form.

*MALT, SPECIALTY*: Additional malt grains added to the wort for color, flavor and conditioning. Crystal, black patent and chocolate malts are among the most commonly used.

*MASHING*: An advanced brewing process whereby grains and malts are boiled at prescribed temperatures and time intervals. Mashing triggers a series of desirable chemical reactions and is performed before the primary boil.

*PILSNER*: A popular family of lager beers originating in the Czech town of Pilsen. Characterized by a light, sweet hoppiness.

*PORTER*: Dark ales of British origin with medium alcohol strength and round, dry flavors.

*PRIMING SUGAR*: A measure of sugar added to fermented (and flat) beer just before it is bottled or kegged. Provides carbonation.

*SEDIMENT*: Dead yeast cells and ingredient remnants that gather at the bottom of fermentation vessels and bottles. Though harmless, sediment should not be consumed in quantity.

*SIPHON*: A length of plastic hose used to transfer wort or beer from one container to another.

*SPARGE*: A straining process used when transferring wort from one vessel to another (usually from kettle to fermenter). Wort is run through a strainer, leaving loose grain and hop particles. Cold water is then poured through this sediment, insuring an optimal yield of flavors and oils.

*SPECIFIC GRAVITY*: The density of a liquid. An important measurement to monitor in beer as it is brewed. Specific gravity is determined using a hydrometer.

*STOUT*: A darker, stronger (i.e., stout) style of porter. Tastes of burnt maltiness and hops are typical; some varieties have sweet elements as well.

*WHEAT BEER*: Top-fermenting ale usually brewed with at least 50-percent wheat extract. Traditionally lighter, and on the sour side in taste. Much of the world's wheat beer comes from Germany where it is called *weissbier* (white beer) or *weizenbier* (wheat beer). Available in light and dark varieties.

*WORT*: Expert's term for the home brew mixture before it ferments and becomes beer. Pronounced *wert*.

*YEAST*: A living, cultivated micro-fungus which provides beer's fermentation. Home brewers should only use yeast sold specifically for beer making – recipes may even call for specific strains. Available in dried and liquid form.

# INDEX

mussels, beer with, 118-119

# ACKNOWLEDGMENTS

This book would not have been possible without the assistance and knowledge of John Kleinschmidt, a friend, master home brewer and owner of Brunswick Brewing Supply in Highland Park, New Jersey. All the recipes in this book were contributed by John and are copyrighted © 1995 by John Kleinschmidt and Brunswick Brewing Supply.

Also, I must thank Karen Fichtelmann Kleinschmidt for introducing me to John and for being such a good friend to Paula Marie and me. To Mom, Sue and Bob, thank you for all your support. To P.H.W. III and Gretta, thank you for all your help in promoting the wine book. As always to Halsey, Carol and the boys – thanks for your friendship. Tom, Donna, Bret and Jess, it's great to have friends who love food, wine and the good things in life. Friendship always.

Without my friends and coworkers at Lauber Imports, Ltd., I would not have had the confidence to try writing at all. Thanks again, Tony and Judy for having the faith to give me this project.

Hamp and Sue Miller, thank you so much for your time, the information about breweriana collecting and your wonderful photos. Thanks to Frank Mrazik for his insights about label collecting and to Lyons & Burford for their patience and for asking me to write this book.

And finally to David, his wonderful wife Georgia, and his children, Sophie and Nick. Thank you for knowing me as well as you do and for always being a part of my life.